PRAISE FOR *COMMUNICATION INTELLIGENCE*

Enlightening, engaging, energizing! This book is a master class in how to improve communication. Morgan's insights are essential for any modern leader or team aspiring to be high performing.

—**Tommy Geary**, SVP of Global Sales Operations at
Hewlett Packard Enterprise and cofounder of
Cinco Coaching & Consulting

Pivotal to leadership success, developing high performing teams, and driving business results, this practical guide provides the necessary tools to develop and enhance your CQ. Understanding your strengths and building capabilities in effective communication, empathy, and listening are increasingly critical to leadership success in today's corporate environment.

—**Deb Sinta**, VP of Global Talent, Inclusion & Culture
at Tenneco

Communication Intelligence presents a simple, clear, and proven methodology to help each of us build positive bridges—while honoring who we are.

—**Anita Brick**, Director of Career Advancement Programs at
The University of Chicago Booth School of Business

Leadership is influence, and to influence effectively, leaders must communicate intelligently. This book is packed with wisdom. Turn the pages, and take your leadership to new heights.

—**Colonel Rob Campbell**, U.S. Army Ret., leadership author,
coach, and speaker

A must-read for leaders at all levels, *Communication Intelligence* is the key to fast-tracking self-awareness and behavior change that will help you build and maintain relationships of trust. The book outlines the steps to get it right the first time with those you influence, and teaches you how to avoid common communication pitfalls. If you find yourself in a hole, you will learn practical tips for digging your way out with grace and elegance. This book is a game changer.

— **Amy Moran-Moberg**, Learning & Leadership Academy
Lead at Amgen Capability Center (Portugal)

The art and science of communication intelligence is the most powerful driver of human engagement, and speaking another's language is the universal motivator. This book will help those important to you feel understood, feel welcome, and feel good.

— **Don Brown**, CEO of DonBrown.Org, developer of the
Human Protocol series of influence models, and coauthor of
Bring Out the Best in Every Employee and *What Got You Here
Won't Get You There in Sales*

Communication continues to be the lifeblood of healthy relationships at work and at home. This book provides powerful tools and insights that help you understand and adapt your own unique communication style for greater impact. It could not have been written at a better time!

— **Kim Ramsey**, founder and President of
The Executive Edge, Inc.

Communication intelligence was instrumental in the success of my companies. The insights in this book were foundational to building successful individuals and teams.

— **Dr. Chris Neibauer**, founder of Neibauer Dental Care
and Abundant Dental Care, and author of
Unconditional Responsibility

In our ever-changing personal and professional communities, adaptability is a vital leadership capability. Within those communities, our conversations are riddled with assumptions and inferences that often lead to misunderstandings and conflict. *Communication Intelligence* heightens our awareness and provides simple strategies that move us toward inclusiveness and belonging in our daily connections.

> —**Catherine Dimmitt**, Talent and Learning Manager
> at Cross River Bank

In *Communication Intelligence*, Hoop has successfully distilled his decades of education and work into an actionable tool you can use daily. The benefits from utilizing his knowledge and skill in my own career and personal life have been invaluable.

> —**Robert B. Eaton**, President of Blue Front Academy and
> author of *Check Your Drawers*

COMMUNICATION
INTELLIGENCE

COMMUNICATION INTELLIGENCE

LEVERAGE YOUR STRENGTHS AND OPTIMIZE EVERY INTERACTION TO WORK BEST WITH OTHERS

CLAUDE D'VAL "HOOP" MORGAN, III

NEW YORK   CHICAGO   SAN FRANCISCO   ATHENS   LONDON
MADRID   MEXICO CITY   MILAN   NEW DELHI
SINGAPORE   SYDNEY   TORONTO

1 2 3 4 5 6 7 8 9   LCR   28 27 26 25 24 23

ISBN   978-1-264-27895-4
MHID   1-264-27895-0

e-ISBN   978-1-264-27896-1
e-MHID   1-264-27896-9

This publication is designed to provide accurate and authoritative information in regard to the subject matter covered. It is sold with the understanding that neither the author nor the publisher is engaged in rendering legal, accounting, securities trading, or other professional services. If legal advice or other expert assistance is required, the services of a competent professional person should be sought.
—*From a Declaration of Principles Jointly Adopted by a Committee of the American Bar Association and a Committee of Publishers and Associations*

Library of Congress Cataloging-in-Publication Data

Names: Morgan, Claude D'Val, III, author.
Title: Communication intelligence : understanding how you communicate so you can best communicate with others / Claude D'Val (Hoop) Morgan, III.
Description: New York : McGraw-Hill, [2023] | Includes bibliographical references and index.
Identifiers: LCCN 2022059838 (print) | LCCN 2022059839 (ebook) | ISBN 9781264278954 (hardback) | ISBN 9781264278961 (ebook)
Subjects: LCSH: Communication in organizations. | Communication in management. | Interpersonal communication.
Classification: LCC HD30.3 .M668 2023 (print) | LCC HD30.3 (ebook) | DDC 658.4/5—dc23/eng/20230109
LC record available at https://lccn.loc.gov/2022059838
LC ebook record available at https://lccn.loc.gov/2022059839

McGraw Hill books are available at special quantity discounts to use as premiums and sales promotions or for use in corporate training programs. To contact a representative, please visit the Contact Us pages at www.mhprofessional.com.

McGraw Hill is committed to making our products accessible to all learners. To learn more about the available support and accommodations we offer, please contact us at accessibility@mheducation.com. We also participate in the Access Text Network (www.accesstext.org), and ATN members may submit requests through ATN.

*To my family—as I have learned and continue
to learn from them every day about the importance
of Communication Intelligence™ and relationships—
especially my wife, Hope (yes, there is Hope for Hoop),
who continues to be a brilliant sounding board
as we encounter life's opportunities together.*

CONTENTS

CONTENTS

INTRODUCTION

Communication is the number one needed competency
in the world of work today and for the foreseeable future.

I've been passionate about Communication Intelligence since I was a kid, although I didn't know the term for it then. I *did* know that I was intently curious about people and how they interact. While in elementary school, I would walk home, stopping along the way to visit with neighbors and learn about their lives. As a student reporter for the local newspaper, I had a more formal process to document and share stories of human interest. When I graduated to the world of work at the local television station, my interest in how people communicate grew, and so did my list of questions:

- Do individuals recognize the *overwhelming impact that communication has* on all aspects of work—and life?
- Are people aware they have *different styles of communicating*?
- Do they grasp *how others perceive their messages* and intended meaning?
- Is there a way to *document the impact* that communication has on employees, customers, teams, and an organization's bottom line?
- Is it possible to *help individuals, teams, and organizations achieve their full potential* and be their best by focusing on communication?

These are just some of the many questions I had on my mind throughout my personal life, but more so, in my career.

At the TV station, I had the privilege of working with a diverse group of talented individuals on our core team. Allow me to introduce you to a few of them and their styles of communicating:

- **JOHN WAS THE NEWS ANCHOR.** He was outgoing and friendly and talked enthusiastically about everything. He was persuasive and able to convince almost anyone into giving an interview. All about action, he really lit up when a viewer stopped him on the street to compliment a broadcast. John was the ultimate collaborator and mixed in well with almost everybody.

- **JUDY WAS THE ADMINISTRATIVE ASSISTANT.** She was patient and understanding, methodical in her work, and dedicated to doing whatever she could to help the team. She took time to explain every detail and asked a lot of questions. I don't think she ever met a person she didn't like, and she certainly never had an enemy. She confided to me that she felt constantly under pressure and had a sense of urgency that others didn't seem to get. "They never have gotten me," she said, "and I wonder if they ever will."

- **BRIAN, THE CAMERAMAN, WAS PRECISE AND ACCURATE IN EVERYTHING HE DID AND SAID**—you could always depend on Brian. He admitted to being a bit of a perfectionist and wanted to get it right the first time. He tried hard to fit into the fast-paced, mostly unpredictable cycle of news breaking and reporting but said he was more comfortable with a consistent, stable environment. He was dedicated to finishing what he started (which wasn't always possible) and sometimes felt like he was letting the team down. "I like to follow rules," he would say with a smile, hiding what I sensed was unease.

- **SIMONE, THE PRODUCER, WAS ALL ABOUT RESULTS.** She began every staff meeting with a new idea, a new story, a new angle. She set the bar high for the team and was full of positive things to say—as long as the members of the team were meeting her goals. When they weren't, she could be direct and didn't sugarcoat her displeasure. "Why can't they pick up the pace, and why can't they follow the game plan?" she would ask. "We have a news show to put on!"

Even though I really enjoyed working with all these people, I struggled much of the time for them to understand what I was trying to communicate. At work, I wanted to be a more effective team member. As I looked around the studio, a line from the 1967 Academy Award–winning movie *Cool Hand Luke* came to mind: "What we've got here is a failure to communicate." One of the more serious implications of the lack of communication is the lack of trust, especially a misunderstanding that has occurred multiple times. We all know it's difficult to repair the damage that a lack of trust does to relationships in our personal and business lives. So, I started to ask myself, "Was this just the way it has always been in every workplace and was always meant to be?"

Jeff Weiner, CEO of LinkedIn, says that communications skills are the number one skills gap in the marketplace, which means that so many people have, indeed, always struggled with communication. This is not going to change anytime soon in the world of work today unless we take steps to change it.

THE MISSION—COMMUNICATION INTELLIGENCE

It wasn't long before my passion for Communication Intelligence became a mission—to create a system for individuals, teams, and leaders at all levels to achieve their full potential when it comes to interacting. The foundation would be a survey to identify communication style strengths. It would be efficient, effective, accurate, and easy to navigate. Ultimately, the Forté Survey would take less than eight minutes to complete; and the Forté Communication Style Profile would be immediately available, and it would be easy to understand with clear, actionable suggestions to get the message across. Especially today, who has 30 minutes to complete a survey, let alone longer than that? The point is for the Forté Survey to be as convenient and impactful as possible.

My aptitude for research and technology, and my academic background in business administration and psychology, kicked in. For over a decade, I reviewed more than 200 communication instruments and the works of the founders and pioneers in communication theory and assessment. These included Peter Mark Roget (as in *Roget's Thesaurus*), Francis Galton (the founder of psychometrics), Raymond Cattell (the British expert on intrapersonal psychological structure), Hans Eysenck (the German-born expert on intelligence and personality), Carl Jung (the founder of analytical psychology), Albert Allport (a pioneer in personality research), and more. While their contributions were invaluable, the technology existed to make the ease of use exceptional and the validity high, and I felt the skills were in place for me to develop what is now Forté.

Building on the work of these giants, and with the help of friends and colleagues along the way, I developed a statistically validated communication style profile survey that was years in the making and remains a process improvement effort to this day. *Bottom line:* Life goes on, and technology has evolved, so it seems with the speed of light. Every day, we receive and review Forté Validation Reports from our users. The day after a Forté Survey is completed, the users receive a validation request email, asking them to rate the validity of their Forté and add any additional comments or suggestions they may have. So just as we evolve over time, so does Forté. (If you'd like to learn more about the research and development of the Forté Communication Style Survey, please see the Forté monograph at https://www.theforteinstitute.com/wp-content/uploads/2018/03/Forte_Monograph_Final_2017.pdf.)

LIGHTBULB MOMENT

In 1981, the Forté Communications Style Survey was launched. *Forté*, of course, is the French word for "a thing at which someone excels," or in this case, *a person's communication style strengths*. As the Forté system was rolled out, both the business and the development model included and sought ongoing feedback from our users so the science would remain current and relevant and not the product of a time gone by. Soon people began telling us how the system was a game changer for individuals, teams, and organizations.

> "This helped us to identify, improve, and strategically use our communication style to lead with more excellence," said Dr. Benny Rodriguez, a clinical psychologist and master coach.

> "Providing clarity and building trust, choosing commitment to strategy and effective communication techniques that promote productive dialogue, better decision-making, and being able to effectively influence others are just a few of the behavioral changes we have seen in our clients and teams," reported Lori Harris of Harris Whitesell Consulting, LLC.

> "There is no better way to assist with the process of improving communication and teamwork," stated Larry N. Long, PhD, an organizational development advisor with Berkshire Hathaway Energy.

It wasn't long before the growing list of qualitative testimonials evolved into quantitative data on how Communication Intelligence, as measured and developed by the Forté system, translates into solid business outcomes—productivity, profitability, engagement, and retention.

Over more than 40 years, upward of 6,000 businesses and 6 million people have used Forté to bring better communication, better collaboration, and better results to their business and truly find their team's voice. Our story has become part of theirs.

I want the same for you.

YOUR COMMUNICATION INTELLIGENCE JOURNEY

First, an invitation to take a free Forté Communication Style Survey. As noted above, it takes about eight minutes (much shorter than most surveys or assessments). Simply go to https://www.fortecq.com/survey and complete the survey. A report will be emailed to you that details your communication style strengths and much more. You also will have the opportunity for a feedback session with a Forté Communication Coach. Please note that this is optional. This book will lead and guide you whether or not you have taken the online assessment.

It's About You

Even if you've never invested the time to learn about your communication strengths and how to be your best at work, you have picked up this book. Congratulations! Your Communication Intelligence journey has begun or is entering a new phase. In the chapters ahead, you will:

- Identify *where you rank today* on a novice to intermediate to mastery continuum of Communication Intelligence, and you will establish your goals.
- Discover your *unique communication strengths.*
- Develop strategies that will help you to *adapt to be your best at work.*
- Document *motivators and demotivators* that influence how you communicate on a daily basis.
- Review more than a hundred strategies and *tips that you can prioritize to improve your Communication Intelligence* practices as they become productive and welcome habits.

HOW TO READ THIS BOOK

No matter where you are on your Communication Intelligence journey today, this book is designed to be a resource and to support you along the way. Here are a few tips:

- First of all, have fun! You will be learning about yourself and others and how to communicate more effectively. You will invest time and energy in your most valuable asset (you!). This should be an enjoyable experience.
- Invest the time to understand the key points of each chapter, and consider how they relate to your personal challenges and opportunities at work, today and in the future.

- Take action by completing the exercises. Research shows that results occur when you document goals in writing. There are dedicated spaces in the book to capture your commitments, thoughts, and outcomes. Of course, you can also keep a separate journal.
- Consider inviting an *accountability partner*. This is a person you can share your goals, progress, and challenges with. It could be someone you work with, a friend outside of work, or someone you like and respect inside or outside of work. Research shows that there are levels of commitment that increase the probability of your achieving a goal. For example:
  - If you have a general idea of a goal, you are 10 percent likely to achieve it.
  - When you have a written plan, you are 50 percent likely to accomplish the goal.
  - With an accountability partner with whom you have specific check-in conversations, you are 95 percent more likely to achieve your objectives.
- Don't be surprised if, as your Communication Intelligence practices evolve into habits, you start to experience the world of work and those around you a little differently. For example:
  - You are likely to become more sensitive to the communication preferences, strengths, and styles of those you interact with.
  - The way people relate to each other may have more significance for you.
  - Your evolution may also begin to influence those around you. Others not only may start commenting about how you seem more confident and calmer, but may even become curious about what you are doing. They may look to you as a resource for how they can improve their Communication Intelligence.

As on any journey, there may be hills and valleys and ups and downs. Each and every step is a learning process that will bring you closer to being your best and to bringing your best to work through Communication Intelligence . . . enjoy the ride!

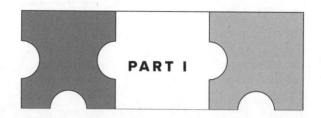

PART I

BEING YOUR BEST— YOUR COMMUNICATION INTELLIGENCE STRENGTHS

CHAPTER
1

WHAT IS COMMUNICATION INTELLIGENCE?

Communication without intelligence has less value.
Intelligence without communication misses out on value.
Communication + intelligence = immense value.

Is it possible to exaggerate the importance of communication?

I don't think so because communication is the very essence of what it means to be human. From the day we are born until the day we die, communication in its broadest and most miraculous sense permeates all that we are and all that we can be. The fact that we choose how to communicate is a reflection of our identity, provides opportunities for growth, and is an ongoing and personal experience. It is how we share information and leverage words, symbols, and sounds to connect the sender and receiver. Communication (or the lack thereof) has started wars and established peace. It is embedded in the language of love and great art, music, literature, and inventions. It defies time and defines history. It has saved lives and helped souls soar.

It allows for the beginning and building of relationships, as well as leads to their destruction and fall. Effective communication enables communities of all sizes and types to be supported and strong, while ineffective and poor communication practices can leave communities undermined and weak. It also is how we talk to ourselves—seriously, what is the voice in your head saying at this moment?

Can you imagine a world without communication? Living as we know it simply wouldn't exist. So, instead, let's imagine a world of work with more *effective* communication!

Communication is one of the most critical competencies to have in a work context, but many individuals and organizations take it for granted since it's a natural part of the human experience. There are those who dismiss it as a touchy-feely, nice-to-have aspect of business and not as valuable as, for example, technical expertise. It *is* serious business. That's where Communication Intelligence—also known as CQ—comes in.

COMMUNICATION + INTELLIGENCE = CQ

When you Google the term "communication intelligence," the first returns you'll see are associated with intelligence gathering—a country's "intel" capabilities, as in the military or espionage arena. The discipline involves collecting information from a variety of sources, analyzing it, and shaping it into timely, relevant, and accurate intelligence with the goal of ensuring a nation's national security. Obviously, this is not the Communication Intelligence we are talking about. Still, CQ in a general work context involves similar discipline and rigor. It is underscored by research and science. It is essential to secure your professional goals. CQ builds on the idea that we are multidimensional beings and are not defined solely by IQ (intelligence quotient).

THE TRILLION-DOLLAR DIFFERENTIATOR

Is there evidence that communication has an impact on employees and businesses beyond qualitative stories and anecdotes? The answer is yes.

A 2022 study conducted by Grammarly, the cloud-based company dedicated to helping improve written communication, in partnership with the Harris Poll, studied the impact of poor communication on US work. The result is that an estimated $1.2 trillion is lost annually because of ineffective communication. Findings include the following:

- Almost all (96 percent) business leaders say that effective communication is pivotal for delivering expected business results,
- Almost three in four (74 percent) say their company underestimates the cost of poor communication.
- Over 90 percent of leaders report that ineffective communication negatively impacts morale, productivity, and growth—it contributes to increased costs, leads to missed or extended deadlines, and harms reputations.
- The majority of employees (86 percent) report having challenges with communication at work, and the primary impact is elevated stress.

Poor communication is also the primary reason that businesses lose customers. The losing factors include employees being rude, complaints not being acknowledged, and customers feeling they have to repeat requests for assistance without adequate answers being provided to address their issues or solve their problems. Too many times leaders believe they have clearly communicated these very things, from the mission and vision statement down to the important information that customer-facing teams need to know; yet this study clearly confirms there is so much more to be done. With proper applications of CQ, this is not how it has to be.

CQ BENEFITS

On the up side, there are multiple positive benefits of CQ for individuals, teams, and organizations.

For Individuals

Individuals who commit to mastering CQ enrich their own lives. They also have the potential to inspire and mentor those who may not have had the opportunity to achieve their communication potential through no fault of their own. In addition to the internal satisfaction that is likely to result as you pursue CQ, there are qualitative and quantitative benefits. And this applies whether you are a full-time employee, a part-timer, a gig worker, or a student, or whether you are on sabbatical or are retired and considering work options. When you advance your CQ capabilities, a few of the benefits include the following:

- Being more believable and convincing as a speaker and being able to negotiate more effectively
- Having the tools to prevent and resolve conflicts in a productive manner and achieve mutual understanding
- Experiencing less stress and frustration
- Broadening your access to job and business opportunities
- Feeling more valued as talents and accomplishments are recognized
- Evolving into the "go-to" person when others have questions or comments

This is not an overnight happening; rather it begins with self-awareness and the realization that it typically is not so much who you are, but how you adapt to others in any given situation.

For Teams

There are a variety of teams in a work context, and most of us belong to more than one. Over the course of your career, you are likely to serve on core or functional teams, cross-functional teams, project teams, self-directed teams, informal teams, leadership teams, and virtual or hybrid teams. If you are self-employed or are a contractor or consultant, your team may consist of you and a client. In a family-owned business, relatives may be the core team. With enhanced CQ, here are just a few of the benefits that teams experience:

- Stronger relationships among team members and a shorter path to performing teams
- A greater sense of shared purpose and team member loyalty
- The ability to build support for initiatives

Ultimately, trusting relationships occur because what was promised by each individual was delivered and the team goals were achieved.

For Organizations

Organizations of all sizes and all sectors—whether those organizations are public, private, or nonprofit—benefit from establishing a culture of effective communication. A few benefits are listed below:

- More engaged, productive employees and improved morale and retention
- Enhanced reputation in the community and marketplace, more loyal customers, and new business opportunities
- A healthier and more accepting work environment where employees feel they are welcome and respected
- A healthier bottom line through minimizing costs due to poor communication

It is always a constructive mix of these elements; yet they are the clear result of intentional personal and interpersonal development. No fairy dust sprinkled across the workspace; "intentional" is the operative word.

INEFFECTIVE AND EFFECTIVE CQ BEHAVIORS

The good news is that we all can learn to improve our Communication Intelligence abilities if we are willing and interested in doing so. To begin, we must understand what distinguishes ineffective and effective communication behaviors.

Two essential elements for CQ proficiency are self-awareness and situational awareness. Self-awareness is the ability to understand your communication strengths. It allows you to understand clearly how others perceive you. This requires your stepping outside of traditional boundaries and observing yourself in action. Situational awareness is the ability to recognize what is happening in the environment around you and with other people you are interacting with or are in contact with. With these levels of awareness, individuals with high CQ learn to adapt their behavior so that their intended meaning aligns with what the receiver understands.

Let's consider two hypothetical examples:

- **EXAMPLE 1.** Someone who is a novice in communication may prepare for a sales presentation without understanding who the people in the audience are and what their needs could be. She presents the features of her product as her company defines them (instead of in terms of the customer's needs), expecting a positive response. The meaning is not received as intended, and the answer to the sales proposition is a solid no.
- **EXAMPLE 2.** A colleague who is more proficient in CQ prepares for the meeting through researching and understanding the audience members in terms of their preferred communication styles and the business environment they are operating in. He invests time to build relationships. He explains how his product is a solution and opportunity for the customer. This communicator adapts his behavior during the session to ensure the intended meaning is aligned with what the receivers understand. The presentation results in a solid yes to the sale.

The following table outlines some additional behaviors associated with more effective and less effective communication. As you study the table, ask yourself, "Do some of these behaviors resonate with me more than others?"

BEHAVIORS OF INEFFECTIVE COMMUNICATION	BEHAVIORS OF CQ
Does not choose to *adapt behavior* based on the situation	*Intentionally adapts behavior* based on the situation
Intended *meaning does not align* with others' perception	Intended *meaning usually aligns* with others' perception
Does not ask good questions (e.g., relies on those that lead to a yes-or-no answer)	*Asks* good questions (e.g., open-ended questions that provide for greater thought and understanding)
Does not follow up when he says he will—does not keep his word	*Always follows up*—keeps his word
Ineffective listening	*Proactive listening*
Focuses on *negative, inaccurate* messages	Focuses on *positive, accurate* messages
Does *not inspire confidence*	*Inspires confidence*

CQ IN ACTION

The test is how the behaviors play out in the real world. Some might think it's no big deal if, for example, you're not situationally aware, that you don't ask questions, or you don't follow up when you say you will; but to others, it is a big deal. In fact, not being situationally aware can limit or derail a career, relationship . . . and the list could go on. This is why clear expectations are critical to CQ, from all parties concerned.

Let's look at two eating establishments—one is characterized by less than effective communication behaviors, while the other is characterized by high levels of Communication Intelligence. In addition, Restaurant A and Restaurant B are located in the same region, and they have similar menus and comparable pricing:

- **RESTAURANT A.** When you enter the establishment, you hear the sounds of silence. Where are the customers? An employee greets you—eventually—and, to say the least, doesn't look happy to be there. She barely makes eye contact, checks the clock on the wall, and vaguely answers your questions. When you ask for water, she says it will be right up. It never arrives. You notice that she appears to glare at another customer when he asks for the check. It doesn't take long for you to decide to leave . . . and check out the establishment down the street.

- **RESTAURANT B.** You drive into the parking lot and see a line of people curling out the door. They are clearly enjoying themselves. An associate is outside welcoming customers, handing out menus, promising an exceptional dining experience, smiling, and answering questions. In a short time, you enter the obviously popular establishment, where soft and appropriate music enlivens the atmosphere. You are immediately greeted, shown to a seat, and introduced to your waitperson for the evening. She clearly loves her job and makes you feel like the most important customer in the world. Orders are taken, and the food is delivered with a flair and tastes delicious. When it's time to leave, you are warmly thanked and invited back. You leave a generous tip and can't wait to return and ask friends to join you.

Would you be surprised if I shared that Restaurant A is out of business and that franchisers are interested in Restaurant B's expansion potential? The reason that customers turned away from Restaurant A is that the staff didn't connect with the customers. You may have had the experience of superb food contrasted with subpar service when dining out. The customers in this case experienced less than acceptable personal or interpersonal communication, and that led to the restaurant's closing its doors.

THE GROWING CRITICALITY OF COMMUNICATION

The nature of how we engage in work has been evolving for years. Long gone is the notion of working for a single organization for a number of decades and then retiring. The average worker will change jobs 12 times. A number of familiar jobs today likely will not exist in 10 years due to advances in technology and work efficiencies. About 150 years ago (in 1876), Alexander

Graham Bell was the first to be granted a patent for what was to become known as the telephone. In 1945, the first modern computer—known as the Electronic Numerical Integrator and Computer—was put to use by the US Army with a development cost of almost $6 million in today's currency. The first computer-to-computer message (i.e., email) was sent in 1969. Then came the World Wide Web, invented by Tim Berners-Lee, a British scientist, in 1989. The first smartphone was developed by IBM in 1994. The power of the technology we use to communicate is growing at a staggering pace.

Today most information is digital and has never been more plentiful. I wonder what Bell, Berners-Lee, and other pioneers would say about the amount of information that is processed every second. Consider these statistics:

- More than 347 billion emails are sent each day.
- Around 6 billion texts are sent every day.
- Approximately 2.5 quintillion bytes of data are created every day.

The challenge today is not whether we have access to information. The critical element is *how* we process and communicate what we choose to access.

THE NOVICE-TO-MASTERY CONTINUUM

A best practice when it comes to developing CQ is to consider it as a journey with varying levels of proficiency along the way. A competency in a development context defines a combination of knowledge/skills/abilities/traits that adds up to being able to perform on the job. The level of being competent is how well you are able to perform the behaviors at work. Not everyone is competent at the same level or at the same time. If everyone were, then Pulitzer Prize–winning author Toni Morrison would be just another competent writer. Widely acclaimed cellist Yo-Yo Ma would be just another competent musician. In terms of the competency of communication, many who want to improve have high expectations.

Allow me to introduce a construct that I believe will be useful to guide you on your CQ journey. Like many other professionals, you may find it so practical and easy to understand that you may proactively use it in a variety of development opportunities and share it with others.

It's called the novice to intermediate to mastery continuum. It builds on the concept that we are all at some point along the CQ developmental journey. How we are advancing is defined by observable behaviors. Review the levels below and relate to them; they will provide a benchmark for your CQ journey.

1. **LEVEL: NOVICE.** A novice is, by definition, one who is relatively new to a field or competency, has less experience than other colleagues, and may have had fewer opportunities to learn and develop. People at this level may be challenged in even routine situations as they figure out how to apply knowledge to achieve results. Novices also are likely to be eager to improve and grow and, therefore, may have a faster learning curve than others.

2. **LEVEL: INTERMEDIATE.** Those at an intermediate level behave competently in routine or predictable situations. They have command of words, symbols, and technologies. They may not understand why their message isn't always received by others in the way they intend it.

3. **LEVEL: MASTERY.** Those who are closer to mastery understand their communication strengths and those of others. They adapt their behavior based on different situations so that meaning aligns with what is being received. They are lifelong learners and never stop trying to communicate in clearer, more consistent, and impactful ways. They also are able to help others learn and understand.

YOUR CQ OPPORTUNITY

What if you had the opportunity to be your best at CQ, which is the essential competency for success at work and life—and which is more important now than ever?

That is your opportunity.

No matter how you have previously conceived of communication, I hope that it resonates that the opportunity and impact reach far beyond words and symbols. I hope you are inspired to make better choices for yourself, which will expand your networks and improve the corporate and community practice of others.

To start with, I'd like to ask you where you currently are on a continuum of the understanding and practice of Communication Intelligence. As you know, you can't plan a journey unless you know where you are starting. Building on the earlier discussion, do you see yourself today as a Communication Intelligence novice, intermediate, or master? (Remember what I described in the Introduction about working at a TV station? Believe me, when I was a young twenty-something working at that TV station, I was probably less than a novice.)

Take a moment to complete the following exercise.

Where am I on the Communication Intelligence Continuum? Name: _____ Date:_____		
LEVEL	**DESCRIPTION**	**WHERE I AM NOW**
Novice	I have a basic understanding of effective ways of communicating at work. I am curious about what causes effective communication and miscommunication. I would like to learn how to improve my communication.	
Intermediate	I can describe examples of how communication impacts work—positively and negatively. I have read about differences in the ways people communicate. I have, on occasion, tried to improve my communication abilities.	
Mastery	I can explain to others what Communication Intelligence is and why it is important. I understand my Communication Intelligence strengths and how others perceive me. I take action on a daily basis to evolve my Communication Intelligence.	

Now that you have a starting point for your Communication Intelligence journey, what are your objectives for where you would like to be by the time you finish the book and beyond? These objectives don't have to be specific or SMART goals at this point. (SMART goals are goals that are **s**pecific, **m**easurable, **a**ctionable, **r**ealistic, and **t**ime-bound.) Please write two or three (or more, if they are on top of mind) descriptors of what you would like to achieve.

My Communication Intelligence objectives:

_____

_____

_____

_____

Have you invited an accountability partner to share the CQ journey with you? As noted in the Introduction, this can be someone you work with, a friend outside of work, or someone else you like and respect. Research shows that with such an ally, you are 95 percent more likely to achieve your objectives.

WHAT'S NEXT?

Congratulations on starting on your unique CQ journey! The next stage is building your CQ self-awareness. In the chapter ahead, you are invited to discover your unique communication strengths.

WHAT ARE MY UNIQUE COMMUNICATION STRENGTHS?

There is no good or bad, right or wrong,
or strong or weak . . . it's just how you roll!

I invite you to meet retired colonel Rob Campbell who served in the US Army for 28 years and is currently a successful leadership executive. He is grateful to those he served with and for what he learned in the service. But like many military personnel, he found it challenging to transition to civilian life, or what he terms an "encore life." As he explains, "When you go into the military, you don't have an identity. The military tells you who you are: it's all issued to you. Then when you come out, you have a blank sheet of paper, and it's the first time in your professional life that you have to figure out what you should do." Colonel Campbell is clear about the first step to transitioning in any professional or personal capacity—"it's self-awareness, introspection, knowing yourself."

When Campbell left the army in 2016, his initial attempt at starting a consulting business was a "rough ride," so he considered casting the business aside and becoming a financial advisor for military personnel. "I'm not a details guy, and I'm not a numbers guy," he says, explaining why finance wasn't a good fit. Then the retired colonel took the Forté Communication Style Survey to determine his communication style and strengths.

Here's what he shared about this significant step:

> "People think I'm a dominant person because I was in the military, and I was a colonel. But I'm not. I'm a non-dominant person at my core, and it is important to know that so I don't step into a role that requires me to be dominant, extrovert, impatient, and conformist. Because I'm the opposite in all those respects. I can adapt, but it's going to take energy from me. I have to fill my bucket in other places.
>
> "And this is where I can help someone else transitioning out of the military. I can say to someone: 'You're introverted. That's your strength. This role you're describing—it seems to me, you're going to need to be very extroverted. So my caution to you is, find those places where you can be introverted, where you can close the door, get some quiet time, fill your tank back up, so you're not unhappy at the end of the day.'"

Rob is a perfect example of overcoming even "self-stereotyping" through knowing his true strengths have little to do with earned rank in the military. He is one of the finest leaders I know from his consultive approach utilizing this self-awareness to situational awareness solutions.

JOIN THE SELF-AWARENESS CLUB

You are invited to join a unique club of those people who are *genuinely* self-aware. Organizational psychologist Tasha Eurich and her team conducted groundbreaking research over four years on the topic of self-awareness—what it is, why we need it, and how we can grow more self-aware. The findings are that 95 percent of us *believe* that we are self-aware, while only 10 to 15 percent of us truly are. That means that about 80 percent of us may be going about our day-to-day activities in a sort of self-delusion. There are two factors that distinguish those who are in the "more-aware" club: One is being internally aware (understanding, for example, our own tendencies and values), and the other is being externally aware (understanding how others see and perceive us).

WHERE ARE YOU NOW?

Just as we discussed earlier, it's so beneficial to get a minimum baseline of where we are before we work on improving. Where are you now in understanding your CQ strengths?

LEVEL	BEHAVIORS	WHERE I AM NOW
Novice	I am aware that I have different communication behaviors than others. I am not sure how to describe my particular communication strengths.	
Intermediate	I recognize that my behaviors have certain patterns and tendencies. I can describe my communication strengths in a broad sense.	
Mastery	I can define my communication strengths and related behaviors. I am aware that my strengths influence how I communicate on a regular basis.	

In this chapter you will:

- Develop an understanding of *self-awareness* and its *importance in more effective communication.*
- Take the *CQ survey* to discover *your communication strengths.*
- Identify strategies to *increase awareness* of how *your communication strengths influence* the ways you choose to communicate and interact with others.

WHAT IS SELF-AWARENESS, AND WHY SHOULD WE CARE?

Self-awareness is defined as having the ability to see ourselves and our strengths clearly, understand how others perceive us, and choose how to adapt to be helpful and happy in the world. There are substantial benefits for those who are in the self-awareness club. Multiple studies show that people who are genuinely self-aware:

- Are more fulfilled
- Have stronger relationships
- Are more creative
- Are more confident
- Perform better at work and are viewed as more promotable than peers
- Serve as more effective leaders who generally head up more profitable organizations
- Are more effective communicators

More self-aware employees, through the above attributes, are better able to prioritize and focus on actions that lead to business success. That means that companies with self-aware employees are stronger financially.

The first step in self-awareness is understanding who you are. Self-awareness is an essential skill that you can invest time to develop. It is also the foundation of Communication Intelligence. Developing CQ is an ongoing journey over the course of your lifetime. As noted above, the benefits are immeasurable when you choose, to paraphrase poet Robert Frost, this road less traveled. You will find the journey filled with discovery, development, and delight. I have personally witnessed so many people who have experienced learning their strengths with true clarity rather than assumption, or who others may have thought they were. No one knows you better than you, and CQ is the gateway to that greater understanding.

A BRIEF HISTORY OF COMMUNICATION ASSESSMENTS

The story of the CQ survey begins with seeds of personality assessments planted centuries ago. Personality is defined as the combination of characteristics or qualities that form an individual's distinctive character. As early as 2200 BC, the emperor of ancient China decided to review the performance of his officials every three years with a form of basic testing. This led to an examination known as *keju* (translated as "subject recommendation"), which established a precedent for decades to come. In 1020 BC, desired proficiencies included arithmetic, music, archery, horsemanship, writing, and skills in performing rites and ceremonies. Hippocrates was a Greek physician who was born in 460 BC and is known as the father of medicine. Among his many contributions was the identification of the "four temperaments," which are the key to many personality assessments known today. They are:

- Sanguine—enthusiastic, active, and social
- Melancholic—analytical, detail-oriented, and quiet
- Phlegmatic—relaxed and peaceful
- Choleric—decisive, fast, and logical

In the mid-1800s, Sir Francis Galton (an English statistician and sociologist) took an important step toward accurately assessing "who we are." His research found that personality and communication style traits are captured in the words that people use to describe one another. His lexical theory estimates that there are "1,000 words expressive of character, each of which has a separate shade of meaning, while each shares a large part of its meaning with some of the rest."

This brings us to the Forté Communication Style Survey, which is the basis for the CQ survey you are invited to take in the pages ahead. It builds on Galton's theory, refines the work, and focuses on communication style strengths, determining preferences, adaptability, and perception. Ultimately, each of us is responsible for the clarity of our communications. When we commit to that understanding, our primary communication strength is the beginning point on that journey to point B, C, or D, utilizing effective adaptive messages at each point along the way.

Artificial Intelligence and Predictive Analytics

Forté is a strengths-based communication style survey that shares who a person is, how the person has been adapting to his or her environment, and how the person is most likely coming across to others in the present. Quantitatively validated, this instrument converts data into high-level mathematical formulas, which are processed and distributed through artificial intelligence (AI).

Field and validity studies with millions of participants over 40 years have produced proprietary algorithms that identify communication strengths and behaviors associated with the workplace. This is an ongoing validation process. In other words, you can be confident that the CQ survey you are about to take is based on solid research and sound science. Millions of participants have credited the Forté Communication Style Survey (on which the CQ survey is based) with helping them improve at work and in life.

ARE YOU AWARE OF NEGATIVE SELF-TALK?

Before you take the CQ survey, I am curious about your general mindset. Does it tend toward mostly positive or mostly negative? The reason this is an important question is that your mindset impacts all aspects of life, including how others perceive your communication. For example, in a conversation, do you start from a position of what's wrong or what's right? Are you looking to find why something doesn't go right, and why it won't, or why it does, or how it can? Do you see yourself and others in a critical role, or in their full humanity? Be assured there is high value in being skeptical, as well as accepting something as is.

I was coaching an associate at a dental practice, and the focus of the session was her communication strengths. Not long into the conversation, I noticed a pattern: She tended toward negative self-talk, saying things like, "I messed up the data entry yesterday," and "I guess I'm just prone to mistakes," and "I'll never get it right." This train of thought is not unusual. Negative thinking, it turns out, is how most of us are wired. Various research studies conclude that we have between 6,000 and 50,000 thoughts per day. And according to the National Science Foundation, about 80 percent of those thoughts are negatively biased. The vast majority (95 percent) are repeats of pessimistic thoughts we have had previously. If you repeat the self-chatter over and over, the subconscious mind begins to recognize it as fact. Self-talk includes the inner dialogue you have throughout the day; and most of the time, it flows without intention. When your inner critic dominates in a non-constructive way, it limits your ability to make positive changes in behavior, undermines your confidence, and lessens productivity.

Here is a process I have found to be very effective in this circumstance. It is also a function of critical thinking: Define the situation; then ascertain why it exists; then determine a solution A and a solution B. Present each solution with two pros and two cons. Nearly every time you will move forward and achieve a successful conclusion. Especially as you involve others in the process.

In addition, here are a few types of negative self-talk:

- **CATASTROPHIZING.** This is when thoughts jump to a worst-case scenario without any rational basis. For example, you receive a text asking you to call the client. Your self-talk jumps to "They're going to cancel the contract. Then I'll get fired, and I'll lose my house." Or "They hated the presentation. They'll tell everyone, and no one will want me on their team."
- **GENERALIZING.** You cascade one event into an eternal certainty. "I'll always be a mess when it comes to the customer relation software. And now I'll never be able to meet the deadline."
- **PERSONALIZING.** This is when you take things personally (instead of professionally) and to an extreme. For example, a colleague suggests an edit to an email you've drafted. Your self-talk is "I guess I'm just not cut out to be a writer. This is the last time I'll draft an email."

The message to remember is that your self-talk is a choice—positive or negative. No one person can live up to everyone else's expectations in every situation. An important part of the CQ equation is recognizing that you are always a work in progress. In most circumstances you can choose to hit your stride, find your own path, and enjoy the ride.

Compared with negative self-talk, *positive self-talk* in a work context is associated with greater productivity, less stress, and stronger Communication Intelligence. It's foundational to being your best at work and in life. Here's a RARE formula to help you on this path:

- **RECOGNIZE.** This ties to being aware. Start being more conscious of the voice in your head. Invest the time to clearly hear the words that inner critic is saying.
- **ACKNOWLEDGE.** Now that you've heard the words, acknowledge them. You don't have to revolt against them or blame yourself with even more negative self-talk. Simply say to yourself, "Ah! There's another less than constructive piece." Next, a helpful practice is to write it down:
    - Take a piece of paper, and draw four columns on it. In the first column, note the day and approximate time of the chatter—the goal is to have a record so you can see the trends and progress. In the second column, write the negative self-talk piece—acknowledge it!
- **REFRAME.** The next step is to reframe the negative message. Create one that is positive and constructive. Write it in the third column.
- **EMBRACE.** When you receive feedback from others, do you pay more attention to the negative or positive comments? Many of us tune into the former and downplay the latter. The opportunity here is to *dial in to affirming comments* from others. Write these down in the fourth column on your tracking sheet.

A few entries on the page might look like the following.

DATE/TIME	NEGATIVE	REFRAMING POSITIVE	DATE/TIME— POSITIVE FEEDBACK FROM OTHERS
Mon., a.m. (driving to work)	I'll never be able to understand the new procedure.	When I can apply the new procedure, my job will be easier, and I'll be able to help others. Good feeling!	Mon., p.m. From supervisor: "Thank you for taking the minutes at the meeting yesterday. It really helped me frame the presentation."
Mon., p.m. (during staff meeting)	I just don't fit in with this team. No one even likes me.	I like being part of this team. I feel good about making a contribution.	Tues., a.m. From colleague: "You nailed it at the project meeting. I wish I had your memory."
Tues., a.m.	This isn't working! I'm giving up on the @#@ procedure.	I was A LOT better today than yesterday. That's progress!	Tues., p.m. From client: "You really went the extra mile to make sure we got the delivery on time. Much appreciated!"

Invest the time to use the RARE formula until you have filled at least one page of paper. Then review the trends. You might pretend you are offering a friend advice as an observer; this can help you step back and be more objective. Consider these questions:

- Are the negative pieces helpful or even grounded in reality?
- How do you respond to the reframed, positive messages—lighter, less stress, more motivated?
- What are the trends over the positive feedback that you have received from others? Affirming?
- What advice would you give a friend if you were reading the items? Maybe to focus on the affirmative?

If you follow this practice, you will help retrain your mind toward less negativity and more positive self-talk. This also will help set you up for accelerated progress in your Communication Intelligence journey.

CATCH YOURSELF DOING SOMETHING RIGHT!
A way to maximize the positive impact of giving feedback to others is to catch them doing something right (as opposed to zeroing in on a mistake or area of improvement). Turn this practice inward, and catch yourself doing something right on a regular basis in order to further frame inner thinking in a positive instead of a negative rhythm.

BEFORE YOU TAKE THE SURVEY

The first thing to know about the CQ survey—and about your communication strengths—is there are no right or wrong, strong or weak, or good or bad answers or results. Your strengths are simply the essence of you. They reflect your natural preferences and tendencies. As my son explains, your communication strengths are "just how you roll."

Given that we have a stable communication profile, we adapt our behavior all the time—every minute of every day. Based on the situation we are in or the people we are interacting with, we choose different behaviors in different situations. When you are at home or work or at a gathering of friends, you may act in a certain way. Depending on whether you are around new acquaintances, old friends, new mentors, or old colleagues, your actions will adapt. (In the next chapter, you will learn how to intentionally adapt behavior.) However, your primary strength remains essentially the same throughout your lifetime.

The CQ survey is based on the belief that successful interpersonal communication can only occur after an individual understands what his or her own communication strengths are, how he or she is adapting to others, and how he or she is "most likely" being perceived.

When you identify and understand your communication strengths through the CQ survey, you can:

- Determine the most effective ways to communicate.
- Achieve higher levels of interpersonal communication, job satisfaction, and productivity.

WHAT ARE YOUR COMMUNICATION STYLE STRENGTHS?

The CQ survey is based on four communication strengths:

- **DOMINANCE** (represented as *dominant/non-dominant*)—the decision-making strength
- **EXTROVERSION** (represented as *extrovert/ambivert/introvert*)—the people and relational strength
- **PATIENCE** (represented as *patient/impatient*)—the action-oriented strength
- **CONFORMITY** (represented as *conformist/non-conformist*)—the systems and detail strength

As mentioned earlier, one way to discover your communication strengths is to take the online Forté Communication Style Survey at https://www.fortecq.com/survey. *Note:* If you've already taken the survey, you might want to skip the next section and proceed to the "What Your CQ Strengths Mean" section on page 33.

However, another option is to take the CQ survey in this book. To take the survey:

- First, read the following descriptions of the four communication style strengths—dominance (dominant/non-dominant), extroversion (extrovert/ambivert/introvert), patience (patient/impatient), and conformity (conformist/non-conformist) that are presented below. As you read through the sections, you likely will find that some strengths are more familiar and feel more like you than others. There may be more than one that have elements that resonate.
- After each description, there will be a series of descriptors for each strength and a vertical continuum bar. For each one, make a mark

on the vertical bar in a place that you believe most accurately reflects your strengths.

CQ STRENGTH: DOMINANCE— THE DECISION-MAKING STRENGTH

Dominant

Dominant people are *results-oriented* and primarily *concerned with getting things done.* They are *hard-driving* and *to the point* and *dislike indecisiveness.* They appear *outwardly secure* and are *innovative, venturesome, ingenious, big-picture–oriented,* and *sometimes abrasive.* Dominant people are *good trouble-shooters, decision makers,* and *risk takers.*

Non-Dominant

Non-dominant people are characterized by a *nonthreatening* way of working with others. They are not forcefully demanding. Non-dominant people will *seldom impose* upon others and are *mild mannered, composed,* and often *modest.* They *prefer input* from others *before making a decision.*

DOMINANT: MAKES DECISIONS	NON-DOMINANT: IS COLLABORATIVE
I like to get things done.	I like to seek input before making a decision.
I'm competitive.	I work with the team to get things done.
I'm comfortable giving orders, telling, being directive.	I tend to persuade or influence others (versus telling).
I'm bottom-line focused.	I'm modest.
I like to be and know that I'm "right."	I'm not comfortable with arbitrary or offensive commands.
I'm self-assured and strong in my convictions.	

WHERE ARE YOU? Place a check mark on the vertical bar where you are most aligned with the behaviors. If you don't feel strongly toward either end of the continuum, choose a place that most closely reflects you.

CQ STRENGTH: EXTROVERSION—
THE PEOPLE AND RELATIONAL STRENGTH

Extrovert

Extroverts are *people-oriented.* They are *friendly, pleasant, persuasive, empathetic, enthusiastic, talkative, stimulating, motivating,* and *optimistic.* They are *good mixers* and *good coordinators.* Extroverts like to *be with and influence people.* They are *collaborators.*

Introvert

Introverts are *selective in whom they place their trust.* Introverts *protect their private life.* They *prefer not to speak without weighing the potential consequences.* They are *originators,* and have an individualistic side that can manifest itself in a *vivid imagination* and the ability to *think things through to a conclusion.* They tend to be *contemplative, enjoy quiet,* and *do not need others around for self-fulfilling activities.* They are *best one-on-one.*

Ambivert

Ambiverts fall in a *middle range between extroverts and introverts* and *move easily within these dimensions.* This movement has very little to do with others. Rather, it is the two communication styles influenced by the current task or environment. For example:

- Ambiverts can be *discussing a number of things with teammates or others in one moment,* and in the *next minute they might retire to a room or office by themselves to work things through.*
- Ambiverts can, *in one instance, be a party looking for a place to happen,* and *in another, simply want to close their door to think about things.* This means that those that ambiverts are interacting with *should not personalize* or feel that ambiverts are moody, upset, or aloof *without further consideration or conversation.*

EXTROVERT: PEOPLE-ORIENTED	← AMBIVERT →	INTROVERT: A FEW CLOSE FRIENDS
I like action and variety.		I like quiet time for reflection.
I'm drawn to interacting with other people.		I have a few close friends.
I'm social.		I'm more deliberate upon reflection.
I like affirmation from others.		I invest time to think before I communicate.
I'm verbal and fluent.		I need to recharge after being "on" when around others.
I can appear to be "thinking out loud."		
I prefer breadth (versus depth).		I prefer depth (versus breadth).
What you see is what you get.		My face rarely reveals what I'm thinking or feeling (less expressive face).

WHERE ARE YOU? Place a check mark on the vertical bar where you are most aligned with the behaviors. If you don't feel strongly toward either end of the continuum, choose a place that most closely reflects you.

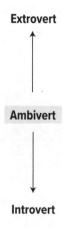

Extrovert

Ambivert

Introvert

CQ STRENGTH: PATIENCE—
HOW YOU PACE YOURSELF

Patient

Patient individuals are *relaxed, easygoing, steady, amiable, warm, dependent, sincere, likable,* and are *good listeners.* Patient people like *peace and harmony,* like to *be cooperative,* like to *save time,* and like *time to adjust to changes.* Their first answer is not their best answer. They like to *think things over before responding.*

Impatient

Impatient people are *action-oriented* and *do not like delays for extended periods of time.* They often have to *do things twice for lack of adequate planning.* Impatient people have a *strong sense of urgency, both for themselves and for those around them.* It is important for these individuals to *keep busy* and *have others respond quickly to them.* They *learn quickly* and *prefer variety* as opposed to a single area of concentration. Their sense of urgency often drives them to *seek out new, exciting situations* that offer a *change of pace.*

PATIENT—IS STEADY-PACED	IMPATIENT—TAKES ACTION NOW
I am generally relaxed and steady.	I tend to be fast-paced—I like action.
I like things how they are (status quo).	I need quick responses.
I am a good listener.	I like finding something new and different.
I have a good memory.	I'm a multitasker.
I want others to be clear about priorities.	At the extreme, I can be like a coiled spring.
My first answer may not always be the best answer.	If you ask me, faster is always better.
I tend to be moderate in taste and manner.	

WHERE ARE YOU? Place a check mark on the vertical bar where you are most aligned with the behaviors. If you don't feel strongly toward either end of the continuum, choose a place that most closely reflects you.

Patient

Flexible

Impatient

CQ STRENGTH: CONFORMITY— HOW YOU THINK ABOUT THINGS

Conformist

Conformists, depending upon their environment and experience, will be *careful, accurate, precise, thorough, skillful, dependable, meticulous, conservative, prudent, anxious*, and *prone to worry*. They tend toward *perfectionism* and are *sensitive to criticism*. However, they welcome constructive criticism. Liking *details and systems,* they prefer to *work systematically,* want *outcomes to be "correct,"* and want to be *fair.*

Non-Conformist

Non-conformists, or *independent people,* are characterized by a *generalist orientation to life.* They often show a *rather independent attitude,* with a tendency to *avoid detailed work.* These individuals usually are *uninhibited and candid,* and they *relate well to activities that take them out of ordinary or prescribed situations.* Non-conformists want *freedom and minimal controls, both in work and in personal relationships.* They can be resistant to controls and will tend to *see the big picture.*

CONFORMIST—TRADITIONAL	NON-CONFORMIST—FREETHINKING
I am accurate, precise, and careful.	I always am looking for better ways to do something.
I have a strong sense for what is correct.	
I like rules—I like structure.	I see the big picture.
Count on me for the details.	I'm independent.
Position, authority, and family hierarchy are important to me.	I'm not so much interested in the details.
	I like more freedom—don't try to overcontrol or manage me.
I'm more formal in most situations.	

WHERE ARE YOU? Place a check mark on the vertical bar where you are most aligned with the behaviors. If you don't feel strongly toward either end of the continuum, choose a place that most closely reflects you.

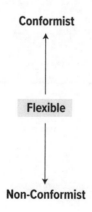

Congratulations for investing the time on this important step in your self-awareness journey! The next step is to discover your primary strengths, secondary strengths, and sub-strengths. Take the four points from the earlier rankings on each of the four strengths and plot them on the table below.

Dominant	Extrovert	Patient	Conformist
Flexible	Ambivert	Flexible	Flexible
Non-Dominant	Introvert	Impatient	Non-Conformist

Now answer these questions:

- Which strength is further toward the CQ strength *above the line*? This is your *primary strength.*
- Which strength is closer to the CQ strength *below the line*? This is your *secondary strength.*
- What are the *remaining two strengths*? These are your *two sub-strengths.*

My primary strength is _____

My secondary strength is _____

My sub-strengths are _____

and _____

CQ NOTE

Would you like to check to see how valid your self-assessment results are? If you're curious, you have the option to take the online Forté Communication Style Survey. Go to https://www.fortecq.com/survey.

WHAT YOUR CQ STRENGTHS MEAN

Here are a few starting points in understanding the meaning of your strengths:

- Although your primary strength has the most significant impact on your communication style, *all the strengths have roles to play.* None of us are just one strength—the strengths work together in a unique way that defines who you are.
- *The strengths serve as buffers to each other.* This means that they work together to contribute to adjustments that reduce stress and contribute to well-being and more effective communication. If one strength is too sharp or loud, the others can round it out.
- The *intensity* of a strength is indicated by *how far it is from the midline on the continuum.*

YOUR PRIMARY STRENGTH. Your primary strength is the *most influential* of the communication strengths and constitutes about 60 percent of your communication style. Review the descriptors from earlier in the chapter. Which terms and words resonate most with you?

_____

_____

_____

_____

YOUR SECONDARY STRENGTH. Your secondary is the *next most influential* of the communication strengths. Review the descriptors from earlier in the chapter. Which terms and words resonate most with you?

_____

_____

_____

_____

YOUR SUB-STRENGTHS. These are the next most influential of the communication strengths. Review the descriptors from earlier in the chapter. Which terms and words resonate most with you?

_____

_____

_____

_____

YOUR STRENGTHS IN ACTION

EXAMPLE 1. Aaron has a *primary strength of dominance* and a *secondary strength of introversion*. It is likely that he:

- Likes to *get things done*, is *competitive*, and is focused on the *bottom line* (dominant).
- Appreciates time to *recharge his batteries* after being "on" around others, has a few close friends, and tends to *hold his feelings close* (introvert).

EXAMPLE 2. Zoe has a *primary strength of conformity* and a *secondary strength of non-dominance*. It is likely that she:

- Likes *rules and structure,* can be counted on to *cover the details,* and is *accurate and precise* (conformist).
- Works best on a *team,* is *modest,* and likes to have *input from others* before making a decision (non-dominant).

Now consider your strengths—are there ways they have served you well and have been useful in how you communicate and live your life?

ON THE ROAD TO CQ MASTERY— YOUR UNIQUE STRENGTHS

Now that you have identified your primary strength, secondary strength, and sub-strengths, the next step is to enhance your awareness of how they influence your communication and interactions. Here are a few ways that you could do that:

- **DOCUMENT.** One idea is to review the strengths and document a couple of words or descriptors related to each one on your phone or on a card that you can carry.
- **OBSERVE.** Then start to be your own observer. When is a strength-related behavior in play? For example:
  - If your primary is patience, do you find yourself second-guessing the first answer that you offer? Do you feel more at ease when there is a steady pace at work?
  - If your primary is non-conformity, are you looking for the big picture (instead of being caught in the weeds)? Are you always asking, "How can this be done better?"
- **ACKNOWLEDGE.** It may seem a bit awkward and even startling as you become increasingly aware of the influence of your communication strengths. Over time, you will fall into a rhythm of being your own observer and noticing patterns.

WHAT'S NEXT?

You will also likely start to observe that you are adapting your behavior depending on the people around you and the situations you are in. This sets the stage for the next question in your CQ journey—are you *intentionally adapting*?

AM I INTENTIONALLY ADAPTING?

People don't change. They evolve and grow through
learning, experience, and feedback. Adapt to thrive!

Communication strengths are evident from an early age. As soon as you
begin to sense that you are a unique being, your self-awareness emerges and
develops. The need to adapt (and it is a *need*, not optional) also emerges
early in life, generally from about when we are seven to nine months old.
From then on, adapting occurs as an ongoing response to the conditions
and situations we are in and the people we are around. We evolve through
adapting (we don't change).

A challenge is that adapting can result in a sense of harmony or in a
sense of uneasiness. Typically, strong relationships, harmony, and productive performance occur when we know that how we are adapting is understood by others in the way we intend. Uneasiness occurs when there is less
successful interpersonal communication: We lose the sense of understanding others, empathizing with them, and feeling connected. The way others
perceive our actions is not what we intend. Instead of harmony, there can be
discord.

TUNING IN

Those of you who are musically inclined may be familiar with a sound board. A talented colleague and friend, Jessica, recently explained how this instrument is, for her, a harmonious metaphor for intentionally adapting. In simple terms, a sound board (also known as a mixing board or mixer) merges sounds from multiple inputs (e.g., vocalists, instruments, computers, microphones). The result is that they can be sent as one signal through speakers to a listening audience.

Picture a flat panel a few feet wide, a couple of feet long, and a few inches deep covered with controls that also tie to a few green, blue, and red lighted rows. Through adjusting the controlling knobs and sliders, you adapt the sounds. They can be directed, split, equalized, and/or shaped before they are blended to create a cohesive signal. The sliders impact broader adjustments, and the knobs are used for fine-tuning. You can take a timid, harsh, or unpleasant sound and adjust it so that it is sharper, crisper, and appealing. With practice, the vibe is smooth and flowing, leading to a desired outcome.

"Think of communication in terms of music," Jessica says. "If you're going to have to adapt, why not adapt to *thrive* and get your needs met in a harmonious way? You need to be intentional. You need to know which of the channels and controls and the types of adjustments and shaping will lead to the effect you want to achieve. The result can be greater harmony through how you adapt and align your communication." This an excellent example of *relational harmony*, in the CQ sense. As the music elements come together, so do we, as our respective strengths begin to balance one another and thrive for a greater good.

I went on to ask Jessica if she'd thought about how a sounding board also is a metaphor for a person who listens to another's ideas. A person who is your sounding board allows you to explore or present what you are thinking or rehearsing. Then, ideally, the person offers a new or different perspective that you may not have thought of by yourself. The result can be an improved solution or innovation. This also requires a process of adjusting, directing, and shaping sounds in terms of how you choose to communicate. I believe this also has implications for how we adapt (more about this ahead).

WHERE ARE YOU NOW?

Where are you now in terms of intentionally adapting?

LEVEL	BEHAVIORS	WHERE I AM NOW
Novice	I haven't thought about adapting—this is a new concept.	
Intermediate	I am sometimes aware that I adapt. I am sometimes aware that others adapt.	
Mastery	I intentionally adapt my behavior to achieve objectives for myself and others. I am aware when I adapt and the messages I intend align with what the receiver understands.	

In this chapter you will:

- Understand *what adapting is* and its *significance for getting your needs met.*
- Identify the *results of unconscious versus conscious/intentional adapting* at work and in life.
- Explore *situational awareness* and its relation to adapting.
- Learn about tuning into *your discomfort zone.*
- Apply the *ADAPT formula* for intentional adapting.
- Put *adapting in action* through specific exercises you can tailor and apply starting today.

This part of the CQ journey is an excellent opportunity *to invite your accountability partner* to share in the ride.

SITUATIONAL AWARENESS

The last chapter on discovering your primary CQ strengths focused on self-awareness. The next evolution in the CQ journey builds on situational awareness. This includes:

- Perceiving what is going on in the surrounding environment and events
- Understanding the significance of what is happening
- Projecting likely occurrences and outcomes in the future

An example in a work context might be a construction or manufacturing site where safety is the top priority. Employees are trained to be aware of excess material on the floor (the scrap material), which may be a hazard, as well as problems with machines or team members not complying with safety protocols. Other examples: Healthcare professionals are coached to be aware of a patient's non-verbal symptoms. Airplane employees watch for erratic behavior among passengers. And a business development associate uses situational awareness to read a client's buying signals.

UNCONSCIOUS AND CONSCIOUS ADAPTING

There are times when you adapt more unconsciously, and there are times when you adapt more consciously or intentionally. This is tied to what you sense or observe through situational awareness:

- **UNCONSCIOUS ADAPTING.** Adaptive unconscious behavior occurs when we process information and act without realizing it. It can seem instant, effortless, and on automatic. Say, for example, you are driving a car to the store. Another car swerves into your lane. You automatically project that if you don't do something to change your direction, the car will hit your car. You instinctively adapt and change lanes.

- **CONSCIOUS OR INTENTIONAL ADAPTING.** The word *consciousness* is derived from the Latin term *conscius*, which means "knowing, aware." This is the foundation for how we perceive and how we choose to act. So, for example, suppose you are an introvert and are planning to work from home. You receive a text that a prospect is in town and has requested to meet you in person for the first time. With the goal of building a long-term relationship in mind, you adjust your schedule and head to the office.

Here's a side-by-side table of some key distinctions between unconscious and conscious adapting.

UNCONSCIOUS ADAPTING	CONSCIOUS ADAPTING
Mental processes out of reach of the conscious mind	Mental processes driven by conscious thoughts and decisions
Occurs in an effortless way	Is more deliberative
Is instinctive	Requires more reflection
Is automatic	Involves a choice
Is less flexible	Generally involves options

ADAPTING IN ACTION AT WORK

Now that we've looked at some of the fundamentals, here are two examples of effective intentional adapting in a work context. One is a quantitative example where a sales team integrated proven communication behaviors to impact a company's bottom line. The other is where coworkers with different communication strengths chose to adapt for a more harmonious and productive relationship.

Scenario: Sales Team's Adapting Pays Off

Stock Building Supply was a longtime client of mine that was headquartered in North Carolina. The company was highly successful in the construction supply sector and wanted to expand its services to a greater number of customers. The strategy was to document the behaviors of its top sales performers, which amounted to 83 individuals. This was accomplished through analyzing the company's Forté Adapting Style Reports. The rest of the sales team would be trained based on what was learned about what it takes to be a top sales performer. The result was that sales increased by 12 percent, which was a significant amount of revenue for the already successful company.

In this example, there are principles that can be applied in other adapting scenarios.

The *adapting behavior of top performers* can be identified, documented, and *replicated*.	In order to be *effectively coached*, one must first have some *foundational and related competencies*.	Typically, it is not so much who a person is. It's more *how the person is adapting to others and/or situations*.	There are *three focal points* when it comes to learning from top performance behaviors: • *Validating the behavior* in terms of outcomes • Coaching to and *understanding the behaviors* • *Updating the behaviors* to adapt to different situations and needs

From this foundational model you can build developmental strategies specific to each individual.

Scenario: Coworkers Adapt

Serena, the human resources assistant director, and Allen, the human resources associate director, are coworkers. What happened when Serena, whose primary strength is patience and secondary strength is non-dominance, was assigned to work on a project with Allen, whose primary strength is dominance and secondary strength is impatience? Let's listen to what the coworkers shared about their different perspectives:

SERENA: "Allen was a natural problem solver. That meant he was always asking, 'What's the problem?' and directing others to 'get to the point.' As a non-dominant, I liked to share. Talking for conversation's sake was routine for me."

ALLEN: "Serena's talking wasn't a good use of our time. We had a job to do, and my role was to find the fastest and most efficient way to get there."

SERENA: "I was doing my best to get through to Allen, and I wanted him to respect me. However, the message I got was to shut up, so I shut down and felt invalidated. After I learned about the concept of adapting, I did my best to assess the situation and chose to interact in a way that Allen would appreciate."

ALLEN: "Serena's communication became clearer. My respect for her grew, and I treated her more as a partner. She helped get to the root of problems."

SERENA: "I chose to look for opportunities when Allen was looking for direct input. I learned to state a problem clearly and with more confidence. I stuck to the facts. Work became a lot easier, and we actually began to operate as a team."

The examples of the sales team and the human resources coworkers illustrate that there are various ways to approach adapting.

FIVE STRATEGIES FOR ADAPTING

Here are five strategies to guide your intentional adapting journey.

1. Be Your Own Sounding Board

Adapting, by nature, involves interacting with others. You can invite feedback and adjust your behaviors accordingly. Others may proactively offer advice (wanted or unwanted, warranted or unwarranted) on how you are adapting, and you can take it professionally (instead of personally) and in stride.

However, this is all about you. You are a solopreneur on this inventive journey, and that means you can benefit from being your own sounding board. I'm referring to both the musical kind and a self-feedback kind:

- **MUSICAL SOUNDING BOARD.** It's your responsibility and opportunity to acknowledge inputs from a variety of sources (e.g., situations, environments, other people and their behaviors). And then to shape, reshape, direct, and form your communication into a cohesive message that is accurately perceived by others.
- **PERSONAL SOUNDING BOARD.** At the same time, who's in the best position to assess how effectively you are adapting in the short term and long term? Who has the unique insight to understand what's working (or not)? To identify which innovations are worth holding onto or which might need fine-tuning? Here's looking at you, kid. Accept the challenge to be your own sounding board.

2. Step into Your Discomfort Zone

I offered in the introduction to our CQ journey that this would be an enjoyable ride overall. I didn't say it would always be easy. A way to describe the outcome as you become adept at adapting is that it will be rewarding. You will evolve and become more self-confident. At work, you will realize stronger relationships and greater productivity. This will take trial and error, and sometimes it will be downright uncomfortable. For example, the intensity of your primary strength may signal you have distinct needs (which may or may not be met depending on your adapting).

If your primary strength is dominance:
- When intensity is rising, your instinct is to make decisions and take control.
- When intensity is dropping, there is a need to get more input from others, to step back from making decisions and being in full control.

If your primary strength is extroversion:
- When intensity is rising, there is a need to expand people considerations and input from others.
- When intensity is dropping, you will want to rely more on yourself than others.

If your primary strength is patience:
- When intensity is rising, you need time to plan or think things over.
- When intensity is dropping, you need faster-paced, quicker decisions.

If your primary strength is conformity:
- When intensity is rising, you need higher levels of detail and focus.
- When intensity is dropping, you need to see the bigger picture and new and better ways of doing things.

Recognize that the challenge of the moment may lead to the very step you need to take to reach your CQ potential. Step into, and embrace, your discomfort zone.

3. Distinguish Between Switches (Broad Adjustments) and Knobs (Fine-Tuning)

Along the adapting path, there will be times when an adaptation is larger and more impactful than others.

- **BROAD ADJUSTMENTS.** For example, Allison (a primary-strength patient) learns to adapt her natural tendency and speaks up more confidently in meetings. This evolves as her motivation to contribute to a team goal is greater than her comfort level of sitting back and absorbing the conversation of others. The rewards in terms of validation and internal growth reinforce her drive to repeat the behavior.
- **FINE-TUNING.** Allison then is in a meeting where there are mostly other primary-strength patients. After the first few minutes when

she is dominating the conversation as she fine-tunes her approach. She invites other participants to exchange observations and shares their comfortable moments of silent.

Both the broad adjustments and fine-tuning are important to communicate effectively.

4. Distinguish Between Instincts and Habits

You may find that a natural instinct, preference, or tendency actually is related to one or more habits, or learned behaviors. A habit is a behavior that is repeated so often that it becomes automatic. A habit can be more positive (e.g., exercising regularly, drinking water) or more negative (e.g., smoking, drinking to excess).

This is because each thought, feeling, and action triggers billions of neurons operating in your brain. I'm not a neuroscientist; however, I appreciate the saying that "neurons that fire together, wire together." This means that when you repeat a behavior, the same neurons are activated and become, essentially, programmed to expect the repetition. A tendency related to your CQ strengths is more hardwired into your brain than a habit. It may take tuning into multiple habits to adapt a CQ behavior. For example, if you are an introvert trying to (counter to your tendency) initiate conversation among a group of strangers on a more regular basis, you may focus on the habit of maintaining eye contact as one aspect. There also can be times when you wish to replace a more negative (or even destructive) habit with a positive one. Effective adapting means intentionally triggering those neurons and letting them fire away!

5. Embrace the Process

I want to encourage you to have an open and curious mindset about intentionally adapting. No matter where you are in the novice to mastery continuum, I guarantee it will be a journey of important self-discovery with positive outcomes in your personal and professional lives.

APPLY THE ADAPT FORMULA

Here's a formula that will help you navigate through adapting. As is the case with any other learning process, the first time you apply the formula may seem awkward. Stick with it, and it will become more familiar and, eventually, will seamlessly integrate into your choices and actions. We start by defining the acronym ADAPT:

Analyze
Describe
Acknowledge
Pivot
Track

The following table illustrates how the formula translates into action, taking the perspective of a conformist (primary strength)/non-dominant (secondary strength) assigned to lead a team of five dominants (primary strength)/non-conformists (secondary strength).

STEP IN THE ADAPT FORMULA	WHAT IS THE SITUATION OR CHALLENGE?
Analyze the need, situation, or challenge.	I have three months to prove that I can lead a team that is naturally not aligned with my leadership preferences.
Describe it specifically and objectively.	As of week one, I am feeling stressed by the unchanneled energy in the room. I need more focus and detail. The others say they want to understand the big picture. I can tell that the members of the group will go their own way unless I can adapt and meet them somewhat on their terms.
Acknowledge constraints and resources.	A primary constraint is time. If something doesn't change soon, I will lose the team's respect. A resource is that three of the team members may not be extreme non-conformists. They may appreciate a middle ground.
Pivot as needed; decide how to intentionally adapt; stay alert; be open-minded and responsive.	How I'll intentionally adapt: • I'll keep my eye on the larger goal of three-month success (instead of short-term stress). • I'll delegate and challenge the group: 　– We'll work together on a high-level strategic plan. 　– The three with central tendencies will work with me on more detailed timelines and objectives. 　– The true non-conformists will be tasked with finding new and innovative solutions to distinguish our project.
Track the outcomes and continuously improve.	I'll track outcomes on a daily basis. I'll ask the five team members how they would like to report (e.g., I won't require their entering data into the online system on a daily basis). I'll keep the team informed by emails twice a week and hold weekly meetings. I'll be sure to ask for input on how this is working and will continue to adapt. I'll celebrate successes with the team along the way!

HOW DO YOU ADAPT?

Now that you're tuning into why adapting is essential and have some ideas of how to intentionally apply this behavior, it's your turn to explore this in action. Below are two exercises to help you practice doing this. The first invites you to take a look at *someone you admire* and monitor *the person's adapting behaviors.* The second invites you to channel the same perspective into *your adapting behaviors.* Choose the one that calls to you most force-fully. (Of course, you can tackle both.) An option is to use the ADAPT formula to guide your adapting behavior.

Exercise 1. A Day in the Adapting Life of a Role Model

SITUATION. Who is a person you admire, look up to, or aspire to be like professionally?

ACTION. Observe how this person adapts in communication and interactions:
- What is the person *doing successfully*? (Is the person incorporating elements of the ADAPT formula?)
- *What or who* is the person adapting to? Are there *general or more specific* environments or individuals involved? Is situational awareness in play?

RESULTS.
- What are the *results of the person's communication*?
- How *can you get the same results* in your interactions?

Exercise 2. A Day in Your Adapting Life

SITUATION. What can you learn about your own adapting behavior? Select a day. This could be one in the recent past, or you can choose to follow a day in real time—today or tomorrow.

ACTION. Observe yourself going through your day. What do you see?
- Whom did you *interact with*?
- Were the *interactions diverse, or were there commonalities*?
- How did you go about *getting your needs met*?
- How did *you adapt*? Did you apply elements of the ADAPT formula?

RESULTS. What was your intended outcome, and did you achieve that?

ON THE ROAD TO CQ MASTERY— INTENTIONALLY ADAPTING

By now, you should be more comfortable and have more confidence in identifying when and where your CQ strengths are influencing communication and interactions. This is tied *to heightening your self-awareness.*

The *intentionally adapting* challenge is tied to *heightening your situational awareness* and choosing how you adapt.

- During your next three days in a work context, identify specific opportunities to adapt your behavior.

The ADAPT formula can be a good framework. You can note how you adapt and the outcome—was your intended meaning more aligned with the receiver's understanding?

WHAT'S NEXT?

Continue to build your awareness of intentional adapting as you move to the next stage of the CQ journey—identifying your motivators and demotivators. (*Hint:* This is probably easier and more enlightening than you think!)

WHAT IS MOTIVATING ME?

Demotivation can spread like wildfire,
leaving ashes of morale and productivity in its wake.
Spread positive motivation!

Why do you start, stop, or continue a particular behavior? Why do you choose to act in a constructive way at any point in time? The answer is motivation. It's a megaforce of CQ. Motivation and demotivation serve critical functions in employee morale, productivity, engagement, and the impact they have on colleagues and the work culture. Demotivation can spread quickly and with destructive impact. It is extremely contagious, and you probably have experienced how the behavior of even one demotivated employee, who constantly complains and criticizes, can infect an entire team. Individuals are extremely susceptible to both ends of the motivation continuum. The key is that the stimuli can vary depending on your CQ strengths.

WHERE ARE YOU NOW?

Where are you currently in terms of your CQ awareness of what motivates and demotivates you at any given time? Take the survey to get to the next

level. It is important you identify where you feel you are now. Simply put—
you can't manage what you don't measure.

LEVEL	BEHAVIORS	WHERE I AM NOW
Novice	I am not fully aware of what motivates and demotivates me.	
Intermediate	I recognize a relationship between how others behave and my motivation.	
	I sense that my communication choices have an impact on the motivation of others.	
Mastery	I recognize what motivates and demotivates and the impact on my performance.	
	I am aware of what motivates and demotivates others and how I can adapt my CQ to lead to a positive outcome.	

Once you know where you are in terms of motivation and demotivation, you have the starting point. Now it's time to refine your thinking and
determine what might be motivators for not only you but others.

Here's a question: What is motivating you right now?

Before you answer, let's eavesdrop on a team meeting. Those seated
around the table are from the sales department of a residential lawn care
company. They've just come off a virtual call with management about a new
incentive program for employees. The call had two main messages:

- Projections for the next quarter are looking good. There is plenty
  of business with a new subdivision being built and spring lawn care
  season in full bloom.
- Regarding the new incentive program, it was announced that the
  company will be moving from individual to team bonuses.

The three team members now have time to debrief and digest the messages:

GERMAINE, SALES ASSOCIATE: "Frankly, I don't get it. There's a new incentive program, and it's not clear who's affected or whether we'll receive more or less pay. And how are we going to handle the extra business without hiring more lawn care workers?"

LUA, SALES ASSOCIATE: "Are you kidding? I'm psyched. As long as they stay out of the day-to-day and let us run things, it will work out great. I was thinking it was time for something new, and here it is!"

SEAN, SALES ASSOCIATE: "I'm not sure about this. This is the first we've heard about the new incentive system, and they didn't consult us beforehand. Have they thought this through? Will this mean a pay cut for top performers?"

Of the three team members, which ones do you believe are *positively motivated* by the news of the incentive program? Bear in mind that first comments made by others are typically top of mind and may not be the final thought or answer. Clearly, Lua is ready to go—conditioned on independence—to make it happen.

Are you able to match the communication strength with the team member?

TEAM MEMBER	PRIMARY STRENGTH/MOTIVATION EXAMPLE
Germaine	**Conformist** • The security of basic benefits • Fairness in dealing with individuals and groups
Lua	**Patient** • A pace set with no sudden changes • A worked-out system for getting the job done
Sean	**Extrovert** • New environments in which to work and/or play • A fast pace with lots of variety

(Germaine: Conformist; Lua: Extrovert; Sean: Patient)

Had the leadership team known the CQ of this team, the leadership team would have taken several steps to make this a successful rollout. First, before the meeting, the leadership team would have provided a reasonably detailed agenda of what to expect and a high-level spreadsheet showing the bonus levels, etc. This would give the three sales associates time to digest the information in advance, so the focus of the meeting would be more on how to get the rollout done so everyone benefits. As you can see, details and time would have played a very important role in both accepting the change and then making it happen. And likely once Germaine would "buy in," she would become an advocate of the program.

A SHORT PRIMER ON MOTIVATIONAL THEORIES

Two generally acknowledged theories about motivation at work and in life are extrinsic/intrinsic and Maslow's hierarchy of needs. So, what are the differences between the two?

Extrinsic/Intrinsic Motivation

Let's look at extrinsic/intrinsic first. Extrinsic motivation is driven by outside, or external, factors. For example, you may choose a behavior or activity because you expect to receive an external reward or because you want to avoid something that you perceive as negative (e.g., a punishment). On the other hand, intrinsic motivation is tied to internal factors. You choose an activity because it has an inherent value—the behavior itself is satisfying (versus an outside reward). The activity is an opportunity to learn or grow, and you choose it for its own sake.

Here are some specific examples of extrinsic and intrinsic motivation.

EXTRINSIC MOTIVATION	INTRINSIC MOTIVATION
Playing a sport because you want to earn a trophy	Participating in a sport because you enjoy it and receive the benefits of exercise
Showing up early for a meeting because you want to receive praise from the boss	Showing up early because you get a good feeling knowing you are prepared
Selling a product because you want the commission	Selling a product because you like helping others
Painting a picture because you want to sell it for money	Painting because it makes you feel creative and happy

Consider activities that you are engaging in today. Is the motivation intrinsic or extrinsic?

MASLOW'S HIERARCHY OF NEEDS

Abraham Harold Maslow was an American psychologist (1908–1970) who is best known for developing a five-level hierarchy of human needs related to motivation. His theory is that the needs at the bottom of the hierarchy (level 1) must be mostly satisfied before one is motivated to pay attention to the needs at the next highest level. As you review each level and the examples in the table, can you think of real-world examples—maybe in your own life—where a person may need to be confident of realizing one level before aspiring to the next? For instance, a person would need to be adequately fed, feel safe, and have a sense of belonging with others before he or she would be motivated to achieve professional success.

LEVEL	EXAMPLES
Level 5: Self-actualization	Creativity, problem solving, spontaneity
Level 4: Esteem	Achievement, level of success, recognition
Level 3: Love and belonging	Friendship, family
Level 2: Safety	Security, stability, order
Level 1: Basic or physiological needs	Food, water, sleep

DEMOTIVATION AT WORK

A few months ago, I was getting ready to facilitate a team meeting of the event planning staff at a hotel resort. The group members were preparing to meet with the establishment's new general manager, who had been on the job for one week. I had met with the incoming GM earlier and was impressed with his track record, vision for earning customer loyalty, and commitment to ensuring each team member is positively motivated and feels valued.

All the attendees had taken their CQ survey. A meeting objective was to introduce their communication strengths and to explore motivators and demotivators. As I was waiting for the session to start, I overheard a conversation about the new manager, whom no one in the room had yet met in person.

"I heard he just walked in and said that the plastic plate holding apples that was in the lobby wasn't good enough and should be replaced with a ceramic or silver container."

"Geesh! How petty. That just shows how narrow-minded he is. There are real problems here, and he's complaining about a plate?"

"I heard that on Saturday night there was an important reception here for local political candidates, and he was working in the office."

"How inconsiderate! He should have been out meeting and greeting everyone! Who does he think he is?"

I stepped in and noted that I couldn't help overhearing the conversation and asked if I could pose a few questions. "Sure!" was the answer, with no overtone of negativity.

"I assume you were talking about the new manager who asked that the plate be changed?" was my opening.

"Yes, that's right. Just petty and nit-picking."

"Were either of you there?"

"No, but Andrea was, and she says he reminds her of her least favorite uncle. She doesn't like him."

I thought for a moment and offered: "Do you think he could have had a good intention? He might be thinking that we should all put ourselves in the customers' shoes and ask how we can best make them feel welcome. It may not seem like a big deal, but replacing the plate could make a customer smile and feel special. Is it possible that was his perspective?"

"Nope. He was just being petty."

I thought a moment and tried another viewpoint. "When he was working on Saturday night, wasn't that his first week on the job?"

"Yes, it sure was."

"He probably has a family, and yet he chose to be here working after hours—maybe responding to emails from corporate, answering questions from customers, and reconciling billing for the month. He may even have been ensuring you get paid on time."

"But shouldn't he have been with the customers?" was the response with a tiny crack of doubt.

My root cause analysis was that the staff had been so demotivated and undervalued by the last manager that their default mode was to cut down the next leader. The poor guy was being set up for disaster if there wasn't an intervention.

I'm happy to report that three months after that meeting, with coaching and an action plan for motivators and demotivators, employee engagement was improving, and the manager was off to a good start.

"EMPLOYEES DON'T LEAVE JOBS— THEY LEAVE MANAGERS"

You have probably heard this finding about retention in the workplace. The polling firm Gallup reports that 70 percent of an employee's engagement is tied to a direct leader. (A majority of employees also say they would rather have their manager fired than receive a pay raise.)

As noted earlier, demotivation is contagious and can spread like wildfire through a workforce, leaving ashes of productivity and morale in its wake. The toxic negativity that demotivating can cause is rampant and downright depressing if you're exposed to it long enough. Any one of us is prone to demotivation and may not even be aware we've become active participants in a toxic culture.

Here are statistics based on Gallup data:

- More than half (52 percent) of employees are disengaged at work, and 18 percent are actively disengaged. Those in the latter category work to undermine productivity and intentionally infect the workspace with negativity.
- Companies with engaged and motivated employees are more profitable than others by 21 percent. According to Gallup's "State of the Global Workplace: 2022 Report," workers who are not engaged or who are actively disengaged cost $7.8 trillion globally in lost productivity—that's equal to 11 percent of global GDP.
- Engaged workers put in the discretionary effort to reach goals and objectives and earn customer loyalty. They are also happier at work and more loyal to employers.

Workers, colleagues, or leaders who know how to positively motivate others can be worth their weight in gold. Like many aspects of CQ, this starts with self-awareness.

YOUR MOTIVATORS AND DEMOTIVATORS—EXERCISE

If, like many people, you haven't thought truly and deeply about what motivates you, now is your opportunity. Your motivators will vary depending on your communication strengths and the situation. Below are examples of motivators related to primary strengths. Review the items in the tables relevant to your *primary* and *secondary* strengths. Then answer these questions:

- What one to two items would you find *motivating* today?
- What one item would you find *demotivating* today? *Note:* Specific demotivators will vary based on the situation.

PRIMARY STRENGTH: DOMINANCE	
MOTIVATORS	**DEMOTIVATORS**
Have daily challenges	Too much close supervision
Produce tangible results	Nebulous answers to questions
Have a position with power and prestige	Vacillating leadership
Have answers and candor in all communications	A lack of significant goals

PRIMARY STRENGTH: EXTROVERSION	
MOTIVATORS	**DEMOTIVATORS**
A lot of interaction with people	Perceives that he or she is not liked
The opportunity to meet new people and make friends	Is not invited to meetings with peers
The opportunity to make more money and improve status	Has his or her territory (opportunity) reduced in size
The opportunity to be a team player within the organization	Does not feel part of the team

PRIMARY STRENGTH: PATIENCE	
MOTIVATORS	**DEMOTIVATORS**
A stable, harmonious working environment	Constant pressure at the last minute
A minimum of communication style conflicts	Too many communication style conflicts
Adequate time to think things over and adjust	Too many unexpected changes occurring
A limited number of last-minute time pressures	Expectations that are too high and/or not clear

PRIMARY STRENGTH: CONFORMITY	
MOTIVATORS	**DEMOTIVATORS**
A structured environment that has few sudden or abrupt changes	Constant criticism
The security of basic benefits	Rules that are changed without plenty of notice
A worked-out system and quality products	A lack of systems, quality, and fairness
Praise for specific accomplishments	No worked-out system

Please note that what motivates you and demotivates you will remain relatively stable for the next nine months.

ON THE ROAD TO CQ MASTERY— MOTIVATORS AND DEMOTIVATORS

Now that you've selected your primary motivators and demotivators, here's the CQ challenge:

- Track your motivators and demotivators over five days or a workweek. What are the impacts—positive and negative?
- Are you motivated to share these with your accountability partner?

MOTIVATOR OR DEMOTIVATORS	SITUATION	IMPACT

Identify a productive, healthy way to share your motivators with colleagues and your team lead or manager, if applicable.

WHAT'S NEXT?

In Part I of *Communication Intelligence*, the focus has been on *being your best* at work and in life. In Part II, we'll explore how you can *bring your best* to work. First up—the difference it can make for you and for those you work with when you bring your best every day.

PART II

BRINGING YOUR BEST— COMMUNICATING AND WORKING WITH OTHERS

CHAPTER 5

WHY SHOULD I BRING MY BEST?

When you choose to bring your best,
you can bring out the best in others.
That's a gift that keeps on giving.

I'd like to share an example of the positive impact it can have when people bring their best to work. Sandra and Jeff work on the same marketing team at a pharmaceutical company. They have served in similar roles for about the same amount of time. As you follow them through their workdays, can you tell who is bringing their best?

MONOCHROME MONDAY

It's another monochrome Monday for Sandra. The great twentieth-century physicist Albert Einstein said that "the definition of insanity is doing the same thing over and over again and expecting a different results." That's how Sandra plods through the day—the same routine, over and over again. She stumbles out of bed and ignores her reflection in the mirror. She can barely remember the ride to work, and she's neutral about another day at her job on the marketing team at the pharmaceutical company. It's not that she doesn't like where she works or whom she works with. It's a paycheck, after all, and she'll make it through another day. Her focus is how to keep her responsibilities minimal and yet contribute at what she perceives an acceptable level. Here's the schedule:

- **9:05 A.M.: INTERN IGNORANCE.** Sandra arrives and heads to her office. Along the way, she sees the new intern, who tries for eye contact with a smile and asks if she can be of assistance. "Cup of coffee. Black," Sandra replies and reaches for her cell phone as she plops down at the desk.

- **10:00 A.M.: VIRTUAL MEETING—CLIENT CONUNDRUM.** Sandra's glad she doesn't have to lead this one because it is sure to go off the rails. Last time, she thought she had communicated a good recommendation, but the client team didn't seem to get it. Today, she pretends to be engaged, although her body language sends mixed signals to the other participants. The solitaire game on her cell helps pass the time; she rarely looks up but is clearly reacting to her phone screen, not the presentation on the screen in the room. She does scan the PowerPoint slides occasionally—at best—which present sales data well below the quarterly projections.

- **NOON: LUNCHROOM BREAKDOWN.** The regular group is hanging out, largely complaining about work, the weekend, the weather, and whatever else is top of mind. Sandra finds some comfort joining in the habitual negative exchanges, which feed off each with increasing grayness.

- **1:00–5:00 P.M.: PROPOSAL BRANDING.** She does manage to focus on the proposal that is due on Wednesday. It's pretty formulaic— copy and paste from another document. Do a few Google searches, and a cookie-cutter proposal is ready for review. She knows that Jeff will adjust messaging for the customer and Rachel will add in graphics and color.

- **6:00 P.M.: HAPPY HOUR (SORT OF).** At last, there's a sliver of light as Sandra heads to a local bar to meet a few friends. The conversation is nondescript. "I can just relax, do nothing, and feel nothing," thinks Sandra. Her curiosity is piqued when she sees Jeff at a table in the restaurant adjacent to the bar apparently engaged in conversation with a companion. It must be exhausting to bring his best to work every single day. There is a rumor that he is about to receive a promotion. She sits up straighter. Wait a minute, does this mean that Jeff will soon be her boss? Moment of reality—knowing they are polar opposites, is it time to look for a different job, or adapt her style to what she knows is coming if this is true? Minimal contribution is probably not going to work.

MULTICOLOR MONDAY

The revered author, poet, and civil rights activist Maya Angelou wrote, "Pursue the things you love doing and then do them so well that people can't take their eyes off of you." That describes Jeff's mindset as he wakes up energized and is excited to head to work. Jeff received news on Friday that he is being promoted to team lead of the marketing group, although the announcement hasn't been made. He has invested five years of trying to bring his best to work every day in every way. He has served under three different managers with varying communication styles. His focus consistently has been on building harmonious relationships, supporting colleagues and clients, and improving his Communication Intelligence to help the team succeed.

- **8:30 A.M.: INTERN ENGAGEMENT.** Jeff arrives early and heads to his office to prepare for the 10 a.m. virtual meeting with the client team. Along the way, he sees the new intern. He has been impressed with her business acumen and positive attitude. He asks if she has a few minutes and, since she has, invites her to share her impressions of the pharma industry so far. The intern would recall years later that this conversation was a turning point in her professional life. The fact that Jeff chose to invest the time to provide positive and specific feedback to her that morning sowed the seeds for the most rewarding career she could imagine.

- **10 A.M.: VIRTUAL MEETING—CLIENT COLLABORATION.** The client meeting, as Jeff sees it, is an opportunity to earn a significant contract expansion. In reviewing the presentation, he had found an error in calculation that will save his team seven figures in revenue over the next year. He researched updates on each client team member over the weekend (he knew today was the client team lead's birthday). At the end of the meeting, the client lead says she and her team look forward to working with Jeff and his team over the next five years. A big win for Jeff's team!

- **1:00–5:00 P.M.: PROPOSAL BRANDING.** Basing his strategy on the success of the morning's meeting, Jeff invests an hour revamping the team's approach for business development. He estimates this will increase revenue by 15 percent and help promote the company's brand. He sees an opening on his manager's calendar and pops in to present his approach. In the next hour, he proactively sends thank you emails and updates to team members, clients, and prospects. That leaves time to head to the gym for a workout.

- **6:30 P.M.: DINING AND DEFINING.** Jeff had met his dinner partner at a seminar on leadership and communication. The facilitator had suggested that attendees identify an accountability partner to work with over the next three months. The dinner is a first opportunity to bond with his accountability partner over common goals. The future is full of colorful possibilities!

WHAT'S THE DIFFERENCE BETWEEN THE TWO MONDAYS?

The examples of Sandra and Jeff illustrate two approaches to bringing yourself to work—one is monochrome with gray overtones, two-dimensional thinking, lack of focus, and limited vision; whereas the other is a day filled with vibrant color, with three-dimensional visioning, clarity of focus, and a total acceptance of responsibility for being one's best.

WHERE ARE YOU NOW?

Where are you today in bringing your best CQ to work?

LEVEL	BEHAVIORS	WHERE I AM NOW
Novice	I show up every day and put in the hours. I'm not sure what it means to "bring your best CQ."	
Intermediate	I try to bring my best to work; however, I'm not set up to succeed by my work culture.	
Mastery	I am responsible for being my best at work every day. I commit to applying CQ in a variety of situations and continuously improve based on what I've learned.	

In this chapter you will:

- Observe the *impact of employees' bringing their best* to work.
- Identify *who is responsible* for your bringing your best. (*Hint:* It's not your employer!)
- Explore the *connection between CQ, engagement, and productivity.*
- Examine the qualities of *intentional charisma.*

WHO'S RESPONSIBLE FOR YOU BRINGING YOUR BEST?

It's a common and natural question for employees to ask. For many, the answer is that it's up to the organization they work for to set them up for success. If that isn't the case, what difference does it make if you bring your best or not? In surveys, a minority of employees report that they are being set up well by their employers. That leaves the vast majority with a cop-out if they want to live a monochrome life. So who *is* responsible for your bringing your best on your CQ journey?

It's all up to you. Yes, it's a plus if you have a supportive team and organizational culture. But if you don't, either you can wait for things beyond your control to improve … or you can assume responsibility. When you do, you're in a position to make changes for the better for yourself and your team.

ENGAGEMENT AND PRODUCTIVITY

Another reason for bringing your best is that there is a proven connection between your level of engagement at work and business results. We touched on the work of Gallup in the last chapter. Gallup, the global polling and analytics firm founded in 1935, is a leading researcher of employee engagement. The firm defines engagement as the "involvement and enthusiasm of employees in both their work and workplace." People with higher levels of engagement, like Jeff, have a three-dimensional, vivid-color approach to work and life. As noted earlier, organizations with higher levels of engagement have more positive business outcomes than those with lower levels, including:

- 21 percent greater productivity
- 22 percent greater profitability
- 37 percent decrease in absenteeism
- 48 percent decrease in safety incidents
- 41 percent decrease in quality defects

Higher levels of engagement also tie to a positive work culture, high employee morale, customer loyalty, and the ability to attract and retain talent. The following table describes three levels of employees: highly engaged, engaged, and actively disengaged. As you review the levels, consider:

- Where are you?
- Where are members of your team or others you interact with in a work context?
- How do you believe *others perceive you* in terms of your level of engagement?

LEVEL OF ENGAGEMENT	PERCENTAGE OF WORKFORCE	CHARACTERISTICS/IMPACT
Highly engaged/ engaged	30%	Engaged employees are passionate about their work. They bring discretionary effort and often go the extra mile in their contributions to team and organizational success: • They have exceptional Communication Intelligence. • They have a three-dimensional, vivid-color approach to work and life. • They exceed expectations. • They are involved and enthusiastic. • They proactively go the extra mile. • They drive innovation. • They are more likely to stay with the company.
Not engaged	52%	Those who are not actively engaged show up to work and put in time to do the job—without passion and commitment: • They basically show up for the paycheck. • They are "stuck in neutral." • They would leave for another job if they perceive it as a better opportunity.
Actively disengaged	18%	Actively disengaged employees seek to undermine others' accomplishments and cut into the bottom line: • They are stuck in negative (and spread it). • They suck out the energy and color and live in a two-dimensional gray zone. • They complain. • They seem to be against any positive efforts, actively tearing down ideas, change, and other people. *Note:* They account for a significant amount of turnover, absenteeism, and loss in productivity.

When you consider Jeff and Sandra from the earlier scenarios, I'd put Jeff in the "highly engaged" category and Sandra at the "not engaged" level. Have you noticed that a lot of organizations tend to focus more on "actively disengaged" employees? There are write-ups, "three strikes you're out" policies, and disciplinary measures. Sometimes these are the first policies an employee is introduced to in orientation—what a way to welcome a new team member! An added wrinkle is that those who, like Sandra, are not engaged are more likely to be influenced by disengaged than highly engaged colleagues.

What if there were a shift to encourage more highly engaged employees? That would mean more people bringing their best selves to work and the corresponding benefits of a more positive culture and better business results.

IDENTIFY YOUR INTENTIONAL CHARISMA

Another reason to have "bringing your best to work" as a goal is that it's a gateway to discover more about your unique capabilities and potential. Near the top of the list is *intentional charisma*. When you think of charisma in popular terms, you may imagine movie stars, rock stars, and notable politicians. The word "charisma" is derived from ancient Greek and meant a "gift of grace" with a connotation of an attribute that someone is born with. In a modern work context, the term describes a valuable quality in business and leadership *that can be learned*. You likely are already displaying behaviors associated with charisma. Through understanding your communication strengths and how best to adapt, you display an ability to connect in a way that conveys charismatic elements. The distinction here is that bringing your best is the opportunity to become *intentional* in this aspect of CQ. The impact you can have on others and the world is much greater when you are perceived as a charismatic person. It is generally easy to recognize these people in the room. It can be more challenging, however, to break down the behaviors that distinguish intentionally charismatic individuals.

IT'S ABOUT COMMUNICATION

Charisma is founded on having exceptional communication skills, being approachable and present, and being able to influence and persuade others.

It is an attribute sought after by employers and team members and inextricably intertwined with Communication Intelligence. Those who practice intentional charisma get their message across to others, and their contributions are welcomed. They come across as confident and inspire confidence in others. They convey warmth and are the people we want as friends and colleagues. In comparison, those who ignore or downplay the significance of intentional charisma run the risk of undercutting their potential. Their ideas may not be heard, and their efforts may go unnoticed.

Here are three ways to heighten your intentional charisma quotient.

1. Give Your Undivided Attention

Intentional charisma means you are *solely focused* on the person you are interacting with and on every nuance of your communication—no external distractions (e.g., no phones, social media, interruptions). It also means channeling those myriad thoughts running through that complex brain of yours into being *fully present* for the person and *actively listening* to what he or she is communicating. Consider how rare this is in the current state of perpetual distractions! What happens when someone truly dials in to who you are and what you are saying? It can make you feel valued and appreciated and like you're the most important person in the world! That's a feeling that sticks and is a force multiplier in building relationships.

CQ TIP: Being aware of your communication strengths can help others perceive that you are truly present. When you adapt your behavior and build on your natural tendencies in a way that makes others feel good about themselves, you will be respected and viewed as more charismatic.

2. Appear Confident

Charismatic individuals are perceived by others as confident without being arrogant or egotistical. When someone inspires confidence, you believe that you can rely on what that person is communicating and that the person won't let you down. A key is that it can be challenging to feel self-assured in many situations, and this can vary based on your communication strength. You can appear confident when you assume it in your mindset and body language. It can also be contagious! You can inspire others to feel more confident in themselves.

CQ TIP. Confidence is related to trust. A truth about trust is that it can take time to build and a second to break. (There will be a deeper dive into trust later in Chapter 17.) To build trust:

- Be aware of commitments you make—and keep them.
- Ensure that the information you convey is factual and you know the source.
- When you don't know something, admit it: "I don't have the answer right now. I'll find out and get back to you by tomorrow at noon."

3. Project Positivity

We've talked about the profound impact of negative thinking on morale, productivity, and other personal and business outcomes. Positivity, when it is genuine, has a strong impact in the other direction—it is linked to stronger relationships, improved productivity, and a more desirable organizational culture. Conveying positivity requires being aware of messaging and being intentional.

Positive people strive to see the best in others and situations, while being realistic. They are encouraging and have a gift for generating warmth. We'll dive deeper into positivity as an empowering skill in coming chapters.

CQ TIP. An objective of positivity in connection with intentional charisma is to sincerely want to help others bring their best—even when they don't see this as an outcome at the time. When you proactively seek common ground with others with a genuine desire for them to succeed, they will perceive you as a caring and charismatic person. Questions you can ask yourself:

- What are these people feeling (outside of their obvious communication)?
- How can I be most helpful to them right now?
- What is the message and means of communication that they will perceive as supportive and will help them achieve their goal?

The impact you can have on others, at work and in life, is magnified when you are perceived as an intentionally charismatic person.

ON THE ROAD TO CQ MASTERY—BRING YOUR BEST TO BRING OUT THE BEST IN OTHERS

Another reason to bring your best is to help bring out the best in others. Too many of us underestimate the impact we can have on those we interact with—whether it's negative or positive. We've just noted the connection between intentional charisma and positivity. In earlier sections, we've explored how attitudes are contagious. They can bring down, drain, and demotivate those around you. Or they can inspire, motivate, and help others to bring their best selves to work. Do you choose to inspire others to approach life in monochrome gray or in three-dimensional vivid color?

WHAT'S NEXT?

In order to bring your best and help others bring their best selves, it would be helpful to know whom you are working with. In the next chapter, you'll put on your Sherlock Holmes cap to investigate the people on your team and identify their CQ strengths.

CHAPTER
6

WHO'S ON MY TEAM?

Bringing your best involves being aware
of others' communication strengths—
how do you perceive others
and how do they perceive you?

Perception is reality. When it comes to your communication strengths, this means that—regardless of your intent—the receiver's perception is his or her reality, and that is what matters.

WHERE ARE YOU NOW?

Before we begin the conversation about what it means to be part of a team, where are you on your related CQ journey?

LEVEL	BEHAVIORS	WHERE I AM NOW
Novice	I have a one-size-fits-all approach when it comes to communicating at work. I am aware that colleagues have different ways they tend to communicate.	
Intermediate	Now that I understand I have communication strengths, I have begun to notice those in others. I try to adapt my behavior, but am not sure I'm aligning with my colleagues' strengths.	
Mastery	I can identify the communication strengths of my colleagues. I have documented ways that I interact with colleagues based on our communication strengths to build relationships, prevent/resolve conflict, and bring my best to work.	

In this chapter you will:

- Investigate the nature of the *teams you serve on* at work and *your role* on the teams.
- Learn about tools to help *prevent miscommunication* on teams and in projects.
- Document the *communication strengths of colleagues.*
- Determine ways that you can *adapt your behavior to build relationships and address conflict in a more constructive manner.*

This chapter has a wealth of information to help you identify how you are likely perceived by others based on your respective communication strengths. It offers specific guidelines to help you map the communication strengths of your team members. It also will help you consider ways you can use this knowledge to build more harmonious relationships and prevent or resolve conflicts.

I invite you to adopt the *mindset of an investigator* as you look for clues in the pages ahead. Sherlock Holmes, of course, was the fictional detective known for his acute observation and reasoning to unlock a series of mysteries. Is the mystery of how you can bring your best self to work worth investigating? The answer will depend on your bringing your own Sherlock Holmes to bear in the chapter ahead as you solve the case of "who's on my team?"

WHAT IS A TEAM?

Humans have interacted since the beginning of civilization. The concept of teamwork, however, is relatively new. In the late 1920s, an Australian-born scientist named Elton Mayo conducted research known as the Hawthorne Studies. Mayo's conclusion was that the nature of relations among coworkers could impact productivity. Feeling a sense of belonging to a team and having supportive colleagues was correlated with positive business outcomes. At the time, it was a novel idea.

Today the importance of teamwork is widely acknowledged, and many companies encourage positive relationships and collaborative practices.

WHAT ARE TYPES OF TEAMS?

Broadly defined, a team is a number of individuals who work together toward a common goal. There are at least six types of teams in work-related organizations. As you review the descriptions, consider how they apply to bringing your best to work:

- Which types of teams are you on now? There probably is more than one.
- Which ones have you served on in the past?
- Are there types of teams that you find to be better fits for your communication strengths than others?
- In which formats have you been allowed to be your best or bring your best?

Six Types of Teams

The six types of teams we will focus on in the chapter are:

1. **FUNCTIONAL TEAMS.** These are composed of members of the same department or same defined function. Examples include operations, marketing, research, IT, talent and development, and finance.

2. **CROSS-FUNCTIONAL TEAMS.** These are formed when representatives from different departments join to address a common or organizational priority. Examples include teams that are formed to drive efficiencies across functions, improve customer service, or communicate a new vision and mission imperative. A cross-functional team may have a specific life span, depending on the purpose, as opposed to being a permanent team in the organizational structure.

3. **PROJECT TEAMS.** These teams are dedicated to a specific project that usually has a defined timeline. Examples would be a team assigned to develop a new website, document a new procedure, or plan a conference or special event.

4. **SELF-MANAGED TEAMS.** The structure of self-managed teams reflects a comparatively new way to view teams. The concept traces to research in the 1950s by Eric Trist, a British scientist, who studied self-regulating coal miners. In today's context, employees on a self-managed team have the autonomy to assume responsibility and accountability for planning and execution toward a defined goal. In other words, there is no assigned manager or lead. Instead, effectiveness is driven by team members' commitments to each other.

5. **LEADERSHIP TEAMS.** Leadership or management teams are generally composed of people who report directly to the chief executive officer or head of an organization. Team members, working together, are accountable for strategy, operations, finances, and the achievement of business outcomes. Sometimes known as the C-suite, members may include (but are not limited

to) a chief financial officer, chief marketing officer, chief operations officer, and chief human resources officer.

6. **SELF-EMPLOYED AND INDEPENDENT WORKER TEAMS.** If you are among the millions of self-employed or independent workers, you likely find yourself on a variety of teams that can vary day-to-day. If you have multiple clients, you may have a team relationship with each one. Your team may include your website designer and accountant. In a family-owned business, it may be your relatives.

The bottom line is that when you are interacting with one or more other workers toward a common purpose or goal, you are engaging in teamwork. The most effective teams achieve the CQ relational harmony we talked about in Chapter 3. This begins with respect and rapport, which evolves into trusting relationships. With trust, anything is possible; without it, relationships typically end in unresolved conflict. Team effectiveness depends on effective communication.

WHAT IS YOUR ROLE ON THE TEAM?

You may have served in different roles on teams over the course of your career. There may be some roles that are better fits for your communication strengths and competencies than others. A leader in education whom I admire observed that, many times, team roles are assigned without due consideration to a good job-person match. For example, let's say you hired Tom Brady on a football team and put him in as a defensive end because that's where there was an opening. Three months later, when it comes to review time, you fire him due to lack of performance. What's wrong with this picture? If you said putting someone in the wrong role for his skill set, you'd be correct.

On a team, different individuals serve in different roles A few common positions include a leader, a facilitator, an investigator, a supporter, and a variety of functional roles, among others. Your communication strengths are likely to shape how you serve outside of a formal title. For example, if you have a primary strength of dominant, you may help drive the team to make decisions. If you are an introvert, you might suggest colleagues take a deeper look at an issue. If you are a conformist, the team can count on you to have reviewed all the details. This knowledge is a game changer for both you and your team. The most effective teams enjoy the most diverse communication styles. Understanding each member's uniqueness is both a competitive edge and a driver of exceptional performance.

THE RACI MODEL

If you're like most professionals, you've been challenged by miscommunication about roles and responsibilities. You probably also have spent time in meetings that, let's say, could have been more productive:

- There's the meeting with no clear agenda or objective.
- There's the one where people who don't need to be there are in the room.
- And then there's that one dedicated to a certain outcome, and the decision makers aren't even invited.

According to research by the management consulting firm Korn Ferry, almost 70 percent of workers say that meetings are inefficient and that too many unnecessary meetings keep them from being their best at work.

A useful tool to help define roles and responsibilities, prevent miscommunication, and keep meetings in line and projects on track is called the RACI model. It consists of four characteristics that define people's roles:

- **RESPONSIBLE.** This refers to the team members who do the actual work involved in completing a project or task.
- **ACCOUNTABLE.** This applies to the person who has the final say and sign-off authority related to a project or task.
- **CONSULTED.** This describes the people who have information or insights that are helpful to the project—for example, subject-matter experts.

- **INFORMED.** People who are informed aren't directly involved but are kept in the loop about progress and any challenges that arise (e.g., the client, the organization's executive).

The RACI model is particularly useful in project planning to get a clarity about who's doing what. Here is a sample chart that can be adapted for your next project.

RACI CHART FOR DESIGNING 2-HOUR IN-PERSON TRAINING SESSION					
PROJECT STEPS	**CLIENT**	**PROJECT MANAGER**	**INSTRUCTIONAL DESIGNER**	**GRAPHIC ARTIST**	**SUBJECT-MATTER EXPERT**
Develop/approve outline	A	R	I	I	C
Develop storyboard	I	A	R	C	C
Develop participant guide	I	A	R	R	N/A
Develop PowerPoint	I	A	C	R	N/A
Quality check	I	A	R	R	N/A
Sign off/approval	A	R	I	I	N/A

HOW DO MEMBERS GROW AS A TEAM?

First, let's address groups versus teams. I've opened dozens of workshops over the years by asking what is the difference between a group and a team. As a visual backdrop I have a slide with two pictures—one of an adorable group of puppies hanging out and probably waiting for their next treat or pat on the head, whereas the other picture is of a sled-dog team in motion that is in formation behind a lead dog and focused on a clear destination. The learning objective is to challenge an assumption that individuals who are assigned to work together automatically form a team that functions at a high level of maturity. That's not the case. Here are some of the common responses from the group-versus-team exercise.

GROUP CHARACTERISTICS	TEAM CHARACTERISTICS
No goals or individual goals	Shared goals
Individual or no accountability	Shared accountability
No defined leadership	Defined leadership (including on self-managed teams)
Members moving in different directions	
Lack of mutual support	Moving in the same direction
Individuals protecting their gains	Mutual support
	Team celebrating wins

WHAT ARE STAGES IN TEAM FORMATION?

Effective teams aren't automatically born. They generally take time to evolve and mature (four to six months in the best of circumstances). There are typically four steps in their formation—forming, storming, norming, and performing. Even if you have heard of the four stages in the past, I invite you to consider them in terms of your team or teams and how you can bring your best to each stage.

Stage 1: Forming	The team is formed, and each person tries to find his or her place.
	• The atmosphere is rather impersonal; people are not aware of one another's communication strengths.
	• There can be uncertainty with regard to one's role.
	• Some people can be anxious or uncertain about team goals.
	• Others may come across as being shy (e.g., introverts), being very polite, and/or trying to impress others (e.g., extroverts).
Stage 2: Storming	This is perhaps the most important phase for team development.
	• Individuals are starting to figure out different communication strengths.
	• There may be disagreements and conflict about responsibilities and accountability.
	• Everyone is not on the same page about goals, processes, and more.
	• Some members (e.g., dominants) may challenge each other and position themselves to establish who's in charge.

Stage 3: Norming	Now is when group identity starts to form.
	• Members are aware of one another's communication strengths as well as motivators and demotivators There is common commitment to the team and team goals.
	• Members start to resolve differences and conflict in a healthy and constructive manner.
	• Members begin to appreciate and respect each other.
	• Effective communication and cooperation are more common.
	• There are guidelines, procedures, rules, and accepted norms of behavior.
	Note: There is a risk that the team lapses back into a storming phase. This can occur, for example, if there are changes in team membership (internal) or pushback or miscommunication from external entities (e.g., clients, leadership).
Stage 4: Performing	In an atmosphere of mutual appreciation and acceptance, the team works productively and efficiently.
	• Communication Intelligence is exercised; there is effective communication (intended messages are aligned with the receiver's understanding).
	• Each person is accountable for the success of the team process and for results.
	• Joint ideas are developed further; conflicts are solved productively.
	• There is effective collaboration and appreciation.
	• Team members rely on each other, support each other, and trust each other.

WHO'S ON MY TEAM?

A logical next area of inquiry is to learn more about the people who are on your team in terms of their communication strengths. With an understanding of your and their strengths, you are positioned to adapt your behavior much more effectively and to enhance your Communication Intelligence.

Would you also like to know *sources of potential conflict* and *opportunities for greater harmony* with your colleagues? These golden nuggets are offered in the pages ahead.

Team Members' Primary Communication Strengths

You are familiar with the four CQ strengths from Part I of this book. The following tables offer a brief refresher. If you'd like a deeper dive, you can, of course, review the descriptions on pages 25–32. It may be helpful to skim or review information across the strengths before answering the following questions:

- Of your team members and colleagues, which would you like to match with their primary communication strengths?
- As you read through the descriptions, which ones most closely describe the colleagues you have chosen?
- Write down/document the colleagues and their related strengths at the bottom of the relevant table, in your CQ journal, or on a separate sheet of paper. A sample template is below. *Note: If there is a second strength that you believe offers a good fit, note them both.*

CQ STRENGTH: DOMINANCE—HOW YOU MAKE DECISIONS	
DOMINANT **MAKES/IN ON DECISIONS**	**NON-DOMINANT** **IS COLLABORATIVE**
Likes to *get things done* Is *competitive* Is comfortable *giving orders, telling,* being *directive* Is *bottom-line* focused Likes to be, and knows that, he or she is *"right"* Is *self-assured* and strong in his or her convictions	Likes to *seek input before making a decision* *Works with the team* to get things done *Tends to persuade* or influence others (versus telling) Is *modest* Is *not comfortable* with *arbitrary or offensive commands*
Colleague(s):	Colleague(s):

CQ STRENGTH: EXTROVERSION—HOW YOU WORK WITH PEOPLE		
EXTROVERT PEOPLE-ORIENTED	**AMBIVERT**	**INTROVERT A FEW CLOSE FRIENDS**
Likes *action and variety* Is drawn to *interacting with other people* Is *social* *Likes affirmation* from others Is *verbal and fluent* Can appear to be *"thinking out loud"* *Prefers breadth* (versus depth) Has the attitude "What *you see* is what *you get*"	Is in the *middle range between extrovert and introvert* *Moves easily* within these dimensions. *Note:* This movement is mostly influenced by the current task or environment versus other people. Can be *discussing a number of things* with teammates or others one minute, and the *next minute retires to a room or office* to work things through alone	Likes *quiet time* for reflection Has a *few close friends* Is *more deliberate* upon reflection *Invests time to think* before communicating *Needs to recharge* after being "on" when around others *Prefers depth* (versus breadth) Has a *facial expression that rarely reveals* thoughts or feelings (less expressive face)
Colleague(s):	Colleague(s):	Colleague(s):

CQ STRENGTH: PATIENCE—HOW YOU PACE YOURSELF	
PATIENT IS STEADY-PACED	**IMPATIENT TAKES ACTION NOW**
Is generally *relaxed and steady* Likes *things how they are* (status quo) Is a *good listener* Has a *good memory* Wants *others to be clear about priorities* Gives a *first answer* that may *not always* be *the best* answer Tends to be *moderate in taste and manner*	Tends to be *fast-paced—likes action* Needs *quick responses* Likes finding something *new and different* Is a *multitasker* At the extreme, can be like a *coiled spring* Believes that *faster is always better*
Colleague(s):	Colleague(s):

CQ STRENGTH: CONFORMITY—HOW YOU THINK ABOUT THINGS	
CONFORMIST TRADITIONAL	**NON-CONFORMIST FREETHINKING**
Is *accurate, precise*, and *careful*	Always looks for *better ways* to do something
Has a *strong sense* for *what is correct*	Sees the *big picture*
Likes rules and *structure*	Is *independent*
Can be counted on for the *details*	Is *not* so much *interested in the details*
Believes in the *importance of position, authority*, and *family hierarchy*	*Likes* more *freedom*—don't try to overcontrol or manage him or her
Is *more formal* in most situations	
Colleague(s):	Colleague(s):

TEAM MEMBER	PRIMARY STRENGTH	SECONDARY STRENGTH (OPTIONAL)

YOU AND YOUR COLLEAGUES—CQ STRENGTHS IN ACTION

Now that you have your team mapped out in terms of your best assessment of everyone's communication strengths, take a few minutes to survey what you are finding. You may have just scratched the surface of the Communication Intelligence treasure trove that is represented. At this "starting point" we can now dig deeper into evolving to the next levels. These questions will help you put in perspective what you found:

- Across the team, is there greater representation of some strengths than others?
- Are you able to identify patterns that help to explain where the team is in terms of formation—forming, storming, norming, or performing?

- Are there commonalities and differences that could help explain relational harmonies you may have observed? Or conflicts?

INTERACTION OF DIFFERENT STRENGTHS

The information in this section will help you dive deeper as you investigate how you can bring your best to work and to your team. In particular, with the primary strengths of you and your colleagues, you are invited to explore how you interact in terms of complementary relationships and sources of potential conflict.

The information is organized according to:

- How you are likely to interact with those with *differing primary strengths*
- How you are likely to interact with those of the *same primary strength*
- How you are likely to interact with those *within the same strength pairings (e.g., dominant and non-dominant)*

Whether you're looking at the big picture (I'm talking about you, non-conformists) or diving into the details (that's you, introverts and conformists), take note of how your strengths relate to those of others. Here's a sample template.

COLLEAGUE	COLLEAGUE'S PRIMARY STRENGTH	MY PRIMARY STRENGTH	POTENTIAL SOURCES OF CONFLICT	OPPORTUNITIES FOR HARMONY

INTERACTION OF DIFFERING PRIMARY STRENGTHS

Following is a brief summary of the potential conflicts and complementary relationships of people with differing primary strengths.

Potential Conflicts and Opportunities for Harmony: Dominant-Extrovert

The following table highlights the characteristics of each type.

DOMINANT	EXTROVERT
Wants to be *in control of situations* Is *direct* and *candid* in communications Tends to be *technically oriented*	Focuses on people with a desire to be the *center of activities* Has a *persuasive, indirect style of communication* Is *people-oriented* rather than technically oriented

CONFLICTS. When interacting, *conflicts could arise because of the direct, candid style of the dominant* versus the *indirect, persuasive style of the extrovert.* Also, the *dominant wants to be in control,* and the *extrovert wants to be the center of attention.*

HARMONY. On the other hand, the dominant and the extrovert could *work well* together by *combining their technical and people abilities.*

Potential Conflicts and Opportunities for Harmony: Dominant-Patient

The next table highlights the characteristics of each type.

DOMINANT	PATIENT
Drives hard for results, *ignoring time restraints* and people conflicts Will *expect miracles* while giving *few,* if any, *details*	Wants to do a *good job*, but *does not want conflicts* with others Wants to *plan actions carefully* and allow for time considerations

CONFLICTS. When interacting, conflict could arise because of the *creation of too many communication strength conflicts* and *excessive time pressure* demanded by the *dominant.*

HARMONY. These strengths tend to *complement each other* in the areas of planning *with realistic time frames* and of *getting the job done* while keeping the *peace*.

Potential Conflicts and Opportunities for Harmony: Dominant-Conformist

This table highlights the characteristics of each type.

DOMINANT	CONFORMIST
Can come across as *critical of others without realizing it*	Wants to *know all the details* in order to check them out
Is *only interested in details* if they relate directly to *getting results*	Is *sensitive to criticism*, tending to take it personally

CONFLICTS. When interacting, *conflict could arise* because of the *dominant* being *too critical, not having enough information,* and *acting too quickly to change the system.* The *conformist* could be *too demanding of details* and *too cautious of changes* in the system.

HARMONY. They could *work well together* because the *dominant sees the forest* while the *conformist sees the trees.*

Potential Conflicts and Opportunities for Harmony: Extrovert-Patient

The following table highlights the characteristics of each type.

EXTROVERT	PATIENT
Likes a *wide circle of friends*	Prefers a *small circle of friends*
Talks a lot and tends to exaggerate	Is *sincere, earnest,* and *realistic*
May *not be good at setting priorities* or disciplining use of time	Wants *more information* and is *aware of priorities*

CONFLICTS. When interacting, *conflict* can arise because the patient can *misperceive* the extrovert as *being insincere,* when actually they are not. The *extrovert* thinks the *patient* is too unenthusiastic and *not motivated.*

HARMONY. *Working together,* they *balance each other's enthusiasm* and can *make a good team in dealing with people.*

Potential Conflicts and Opportunities for Harmony: Extrovert-Conformist

The following table highlights the characteristics of each type.

EXTROVERT	CONFORMIST
Wants *to talk a lot* but is *neither technical nor systematic* in approach to work and/or life. Is not good with writing out details and would *rather verbalize* Is *not disciplined*	Wants *accurate, systematic approach* to things Is very disciplined and prefers to have *details in writing* *Does not like stories and elaborate excuses*

CONFLICTS. When interacting, *conflict* can arise from the *extrovert's flamboyant oral style* of communicating and the *conformist's desire for factual data* and for things to be *in writing.*

HARMONY. They can *work well together,* as the *conformist* will add a *disciplined, detailed, orderly approach* while the *extrovert* will add an *exciting people orientation* to the situation.

Potential Conflicts and Opportunities for Harmony: Patient-Conformist

The table highlights the characteristics of each type.

PATIENT	CONFORMIST
Is *easygoing* and *not goal-oriented,* is a *slow starter* who is *reluctant to act* May *compromise too readily* and give in when he or she should not	Tends to be *intense about life* and getting things done and *done right* Is *strong on principles,* will *sometimes resist change* without good reason

CONFLICTS. When interacting, *conflict* can arise because the *patient seems to be too easygoing* while the *conformist* is *too intense.* The *conformist* may think the *patient vacillates too easily.*

HARMONY. These traits *complement* one another in that the *conformist gives more intensity and discipline* while the *patient will have a calming effect* while prioritizing activities, and they will find shortcuts to getting things done. Both *respond well to strong leadership*.

INTERACTION OF THE SAME PRIMARY STRENGTHS

Following is a brief summary of the potential conflicts and complementary relationships of people with the same primary strengths.

Dominant with Dominant

Because of a desire to be in control and make decisions, two dominants at the same level may be in periodic, if not continual, *conflict over who will be in control*. Also, because of the *candid, direct communication style*, there could be *severe verbal encounters*. To avoid this, *ground rules* regarding the relationship of the parties must be *clearly defined ahead of time*. Dominants will *work for someone else as long as they respect the other person*. However, even then there may be times when *they will challenge the leadership*.

Extrovert with Extrovert

Extroverts will usually *work well together*. However, because they like to talk, *not much may get done due to excess verbal interaction*. Also, since they like to be the *center of attention*, they may spend too much time and effort *competing for that position*. Since they are *not technical* by nature, they could be *in trouble unless adequate technical support is supplied*.

Patient with Patient

Since they are *not basically demanding*, tend to be *deliberate*, and *want strong leadership*, patients will *probably get along well* with one another. However, they may not be sufficiently productive unless a pace is set by someone else.

Conformist with Conformist

Conformists will tend to *get along well together unless their perceptions of what is "right" and "fair" are different,* and then there could be some definite conflicts. Also, since they are naturally skeptical and resistant to change , they could *fall behind the times because of their lack of a big-picture orientation.*

INTERACTION OF OPPOSITE STRENGTHS WITHIN A CONTINUUM

Following is a brief summary of the potential conflicts and complementary relationships of people with opposite primary strengths.

Dominant with Non-Dominant

The *non-dominant* may tend *to think the dominant* is a know-it-all who is *too abrupt and rude.* On the other hand, the non-dominant will *like* the fact that the *dominant* is a *decision maker* and *strong leader.* If the *non-dominant is in charge,* the *dominant may be frustrated* because *decisions* are made *too slowly* and the *non-dominant is not candid and direct enough in communications.*

Extrovert with Introvert

The *extrovert* may think the *introvert is somewhat reserved, unfriendly,* and *unenthusiastic.* The *introvert* may think the *extrovert* is somewhat *insincere* and *talks too much.*

Patient with Impatient

The *patient* person may *perceive the impatient* person as someone *who jumps from one thing to another, never finishes* anything, *and runs off* before laying out a plan of action. The *impatient* may see the *patient as too slow and deliberate,* possibly *lazy,* and *boring* because of too much routine.

Conformist with Non-Conformist

The *conformist* may see the *non-conformist* as being *too loose with details* and *unreliable* and never getting things done. The *conformist* is also bothered because the *non-conformist resists going by the book.* The *non-conformist* may see the *conformist* as being in a rut, *too reserved,* too *demanding of perfection,* and *not flexible enough.*

ON THE ROAD TO CQ MASTERY— WHO'S ON YOUR TEAM?

You now should have a set of clues to help you solve the CQ-team mystery, including:

- A map of the communication strengths of your team
- Intelligence on how you are likely to be perceived by others depending on if you have similar or different primary strengths

Prioritize

A next step is to *prioritize*—to focus in on one or two colleagues to apply the results of your investigation. Select a relatively short time period, and if it is comfortable, become curious about the results:

- Are you able to improve the effectiveness of your communication?
- Are you better positioned to bring your best self to work and for your team?

Here's a sample template you can use to jot down your answers.

COLLEAGUE	COLLEAGUE'S PRIMARY STRENGTH	MY PRIMARY STRENGTH	POTENTIAL SOURCES OF CONFLICT
OPPORTUNITIES FOR HARMONY	MY STRATEGIES/ ACTION STEPS	DATE ACTION TAKEN/RESULT(S)	

WHAT'S NEXT?

What does the resiliency zone have to do with bringing your best? The next chapter addresses this important question.

HOW DO I BRING MY BEST?

When you adopt the approach that challenging situations
are opportunities to grow your CQ,
work and life are more rewarding.

You've probably heard someone described as being "wound too tight." This generally means that the person is exceptionally tense or on edge. You may also have heard someone described as being "too laid back" or "loosey-goosey," which means the person doesn't seem to have any interest in doing anything except chilling. While there may be times when being wound too tight or loose are useful physical postures or mindsets, it's important to find the right balance between the extremes as a prerequisite to bringing your best to work.

To drive home the metaphors, I invite you to try this exercise:

- First, make a tight fist (it doesn't matter which hand you choose). Squeeze your hand tighter and tighter. And now hold it for a count of 10, maintaining as tight a grip as you possibly can. Then let it go. Take a few breaths.

- Now, let your hand hang loose with no pressure. It's relaxed and just sitting on your lap, resting on a table, or hanging by your side. Let it be for about 10 seconds. Then shake it out and take a few breaths.

The lesson is that it's improbable that your hand could perform an intended function in either of the extremes. Would you be able to effectively grip a pen? Hold a hammer? Or in the case of those of us who attempt the game of golf, have the right grip on a club?

The mindset for this chapter is somewhere on the continuum between too tight and too relaxed that will prepare you to focus, have an open mind, and determine how to bring your best to work. To paraphrase the life lesson learned by Goldilocks, the heroine of the famous nineteenth-century British fairy tale, there is a place that is not too tight and not too loose—it is just right. Where is that mindset for you at the present time?

WHERE ARE YOU NOW?

Before we dive in, where are you currently in terms of knowing how to bring your best?

LEVEL	DESCRIPTORS	WHERE I AM NOW
Novice	I have the basics covered—communication, adaptability, intentional charisma. Is there more?	
Intermediate	I apply proven strategies to bring my best. They seem to work in most situations.	
Mastery	I have personalized strategies that leverage my communication strengths. I continually adapt to improve on bringing my best to work.	

In this chapter you will:

- Confirm that *communication and adaptability are essential competencies* for success in work and life.
- Identify *five power skill strategies* to apply and bring your best to work.
- Recognize the *value of building confidence* in yourself and others.

CQ POWER SKILLS

I founded The Forté Institute in the 1970s, knowing that communication and adaptability are two essential competencies for being your best in work and life. Over the years, research has supported this conclusion. For example, Duarte (a leading firm on communication) concluded in its "Learning & Development Annual Trends Survey 2022" that one power skill had emerged as more important than any other across sectors and occupations—communication. This was followed by adaptability. The survey report states that "while prioritization of skills varies by function, the consensus is that communication is the top power skill for anyone in the workplace, followed by adaptability."

Below are five power skills strategies that are foundational to bringing your best to work. They support the CQ power skills of communication and adaptability and set the stage for the 10 CQ essentials coming up in Part III of this book. The five are:

- Having a resiliency zone
- Building and interpreting confidence in yourself and others
- Meeting goals
- Applying solutions thinking
- Focusing on the best in others

FIVE POWER SKILL STRATEGIES

1. Having a Resiliency Zone

From the founding of The Forté Institute more than four decades ago, the quality of resilience has been an integral part of how clients achieve better communication and better results.

The *Journal of Advanced Nursing* defines "resilience" as "the ability of an individual to adjust to adversity, maintain equilibrium, retain some sense of control over their environment and continue to move in a positive manner." In other words, when you fall, you get back up again and grow stronger than ever through the experience. Anyone who's been involved in sports or athletics knows that the way to build physical resilience starts with tearing down muscle. If you lift weights on a regular basis, muscles grow stronger and more resilient over time.

Stamina in the Zone

It's never easy when life presents setbacks. Work-related challenges are certain to test our resilience—miscommunication and lack of communication are near the top of the list. These occurrences are inevitable, and how we respond to them is an essential part of how we grow, develop, survive, and thrive. In other words, resilience is a prime part of being our best selves at work.

Let's say you are moving through the day, focused on a project, and making progress when you hit a roadblock—a colleague tells you that a needed part will be delayed due to supply chain issues. There are some days when you will be tempted to leave early, with work in the rearview mirror. On other days, you remain motivated and explore options well into the evening. What's the difference between the two times? The answer is having a resiliency zone.

And a key factor in the zone is your stamina level. This is the ability to sustain prolonged physical or mental effort. In a work context, someone who has a high level of stamina will be able to perform effectively day after day given regular challenges of the job.

When miscommunication and stress levels rise, stamina drops, and so does your ability to achieve your goals or bounce back from adversity. When you close communication gaps, stamina levels rise, and so does your resiliency. A key result of effective CQ is achieving and/or maintaining higher levels of resilience. When you adopt the approach that challenging situations are opportunities to grow your CQ, work and life are more rewarding.

2. Building and Interpreting Confidence in Yourself and Others

Let's start by exploring the idea of self-confidence. Self-confidence is the belief that you are capable of achieving goals that you set for yourself. It is having confidence in your perceptions, decisions, skills, and abilities. It also ties to your ability to be resilient when faced with challenges and adversity.

In comparison, lack of self-confidence is marked by occasions when you question whether you are able to achieve a goal or accomplish a task. This can be accompanied by feelings of uncertainty and inadequacy as well as a hesitancy to take action.

At work, you may feel more confident in some situations and with some tasks than others. This can tie to having the knowledge, capabilities, and experience that will lead to success on the job.

Building Your Self-Confidence

Regardless of where you are now, we can all benefit from a self-confidence boost. Here are a few tips to support this objective:

- **REPLAY PAST WINS.** Many of us focus more frequently and vividly on the times we thought we failed or let others down than on the numerous times we succeeded (it's our brain's negative bias again). What are the times when *you did it*? Let those accomplishments sink in as events that you can, and should, be proud of and that no one can take away from you.
- **PRACTICE, PRACTICE, PRACTICE.** Preparation is key to success. When you identify a skill that is required for successful performance and aren't certain of your proficiency, then practice. As your capabilities grow, so will your confidence.
- **ACHIEVE A GOAL.** Confidence grows as you accomplish and get things done.
  - Start with setting a challenging, meaningful, and achievable goal for yourself. Be specific, and write it down.
  - Have a clear vision of what success looks like and would mean to you.
  - Start with small steps.
  - Soften any negative self-talk (this was mentioned in Chapter 2), and congratulate yourself for every win.
  - Invite another—maybe your accountability partner—to be your check-in support team.
  - Celebrate your success—you did it!

Interpreting Confidence

Confidence is not a one-size-fits-all commodity. It can be interpreted—or misinterpreted—if you just go by communication strengths. The introvert, for example, may invest time to deliberate before offering a recommendation. A first answer given by one whose primary strength is patient may not be their best or last response. To a CQ novice, these tendencies may be interpreted as signs of weakness or lack of confidence. On the other hand, one who is dominant may tend to give orders and be competitive—and as a result may be thought of as arrogant instead of confident.

CQ TIP. Interpret another's level of confidence based on that person's behavior and accomplishments in his or her terms, not on your first impression.

Helping Build Confidence in Others

One way to bring your best to work is to help build the confidence of colleagues. Only they are responsible for the outcome; however, your actions can help set them up for a confidence lift:

- **OFFER A COMPLIMENT.** Make it specific and timely. Be sincere in how you communicate it, and invest the time to ensure that it sinks in and to answer any related questions. How do you feel when someone asks you for a moment of your time and then pays you a compliment? It can make your day!
- **BE THE MOTIVATOR.** If you don't already know, ask what motivates your colleagues and then do what you can to be their motivator.
- **ASK THEIR OPINION . . . AND THEN LISTEN.** People feel valued when what they think matters and when they can make a contribution. When you ask for their opinion and (again) listen all the way through to their answer, you will help build their confidence.
- **CHALLENGE THEM.** You may see potential that they haven't (yet) realized in themselves. Ask about their vision for the future—what is their ideal career path? Is there an assignment they would like to take on? You can encourage them to go for it or, if you are so positioned, take action to help make it happen.

3. Meeting Goals

There are different qualities related to goals. I'm an advocate of CQ goals that are SMART (specific, measurable, actionable, relevant, realistic, and time-bound). Even if the objective was set by someone else or the team, it's a big plus if it's a goal that you are passionate about or can find a legitimate way to buy into.

For those who need convincing, some of the benefits of CQ goals include the following:

- **GIVING YOU MORE CONTROL IN LIFE.** With goals, you have a direction and road map that can help deflect obstacles that rock you.
- **INCREASING YOUR CONFIDENCE.** As noted above, self-confidence comes from accomplishments such as meeting a defined goal.
- **BUILDING EFFECTIVE TEAMS AND HARMONIOUS RELATIONSHIPS.** With shared goals, you have common ground with others.
- **STRENGTHENING COMMUNICATION.** The common vision established by a goal can focus communication on the progress ahead and the accomplishments you achieve together.

Another way to ensure your goals are at a high CQ level is to apply solutions thinking.

4. Using Solutions Thinking

Are most people you know focused on *problems*, or are they focused on *solutions*? A traditional business acumen is problem solving. However, the challenge with this strategy is that in order to be effective, an employee focuses on what is going wrong, scrutinizing the weaknesses and everything that feeds into the problem.

Then there is *solutions thinking*. This practice centers on what's going right (instead of what's going wrong), sees challenges as opportunities (instead of weaknesses), and focuses on solutions (instead of problems).

I am a longtime advocate of solutions thinking because I have seen the positive impacts it can have on teams' productivity and how it can help employees bring their best to work. It is a positive and practical way of moving forward and expanding innovative thinking. Here are a few proven steps to advance solutions thinking:

- **FOCUS ON A SOLUTION (SKIP THE PROBLEM).** A huge shift occurs when you focus on the solution as the goal. If the members of a team are focused on the problem, then that's what they think about, talk about, and close in on. If they embrace solutions thinking, a broader world of possibilities opens up, inviting options that wouldn't have even occurred in the problem-dwelling world. Here's an example of how to reframe a challenge:
  - **Challenge.** There is a leak in the kitchen sink.
    - *Problem-solving thinking.* I need to fix the leak (even if it's been the third time this month).
    - *Solutions thinking.* Why is the sink leaking? I'll have to weigh whether it's more effective to fix the sink myself or call a plumber. Eventually, there will be a new sink —it's not a matter of if, but when. I'll investigate the options and the best timing for a new purchase.
- **BE OPEN TO POSSIBILITIES.** Sometimes our area of expertise can get in the way of being open to solutions. Put aside your tried-and-true problem-solving methods. Research different options. Invite those people with different perspectives to offer ideas.
- **STOP FOCUSING ON WHAT DOESN'T WORK.** If you focus solely and repetitively on what doesn't work (e.g., the leaky sink), you are likely to be oblivious to what does work. What works? Why does it work? How can we make it happen?
- **FIND WHAT WORKS—AND DO MORE OF IT.** A full solution may not be apparent right away. However, when you find that promising thread, keep pulling on it until you find the next probable answer. Then keep going until a solution is apparent, tested, and implemented.

5. Focusing on the Best in Others

Here's another example of a strategy that is a force multiplier of value when you apply it as part of bringing your best to work. Which makes you feel better about yourself and motivated to perform: when someone focuses on a negative aspect of your efforts or when someone offers a positive observation? Of course, you prefer to receive the affirmative feedback.

We've talked about the negative bias we can have toward ourselves. Well, research shows that many of us also tend to have a negative bias when it comes to our impressions of others. But through focused behavior, we can train our brains to focus on the best in others.

When you concentrate on the best and have this as the basis for what and how you communicate, people are happier and like to be around you. It can be contagious, and they can spread positive observations to others. It will come around, and you can take pride in being part of a more affirming and productive environment. As is the case with intentional charisma, which we discussed earlier, it also means that bringing your best to work can change someone else's life for the better.

CQ TIP. You have a list of colleagues and their primary strengths. This can be a beginning framework for appreciating the unique value each one gives and has to offer.

ON THE ROAD TO CQ MASTERY— HOW TO BRING YOUR BEST TO WORK

The five power skills strategies are foundational to bringing your best to work. The next step is to determine how to prioritize them and visualize how they can make a difference in your experience:

- Which one of the five power strategies would you like to apply first?
    - Having a resiliency zone
    - Building and interpreting confidence
    - Meeting goals

- ◦ Using solutions thinking
- ◦ Focusing on the best in others
- Write your answer on a Post-it Note with today's date, and place the note where it will be a reminder to apply what you've written.
- Remember the context of bringing your best to work and improving your Communication Intelligence and that of others.

Share with your accountability partner the strategy you've chosen to apply—and invite your partner to choose one, too.

WHAT'S NEXT?

Get ready to learn about the CQ 10—essential skill areas for you to learn about and apply to improve your Communication Intelligence.

PART III

MEET THE
CQ 10 ESSENTIALS

The CQ 10 essentials offer a road map to become even more proficient at being your best and bringing your best to work and life.

In Part I, we explored the importance of self-awareness and Communication Intelligence. A focus was on identifying your communication strengths. Situational awareness was emphasized in the context of how you adapt your behavior to ensure your intended communication is aligned with what listeners perceive.

In Part II, we discovered the communication strengths of your colleagues and how you can apply the CQ skills of communication and adaptability while highlighting intentional charisma. This section included power skills strategies that you can apply.

In Part III, we cover the CQ 10 essentials, giving an in-depth look at what it takes to become even more proficient at effective communication.

PRIORITIZING THE CQ 10

In each chapter ahead, you will find tips and strategies to advance you on the road to CQ mastery. Each chapter is a stand-alone bite. There also are common ingredients that are folded in throughout, such as references to communication strengths.

You may also find that some essentials are timely and relevant for you now, and you may want to do a deeper dive into these. Then there are others you may return to at a future time when, for example, you would like advice on how to give and receive feedback, communicate with challenging people, crystallize non-verbal communication, and much more. This is a whatever-works process. You will find value in revisiting these chapters as needed on your journey.

WHERE ARE YOU NOW?

By now, you are familiar with proficiency levels (novice, intermediate, mastery). You've probably guessed that the next step related to the CQ 10 is to consider where you currently are on the continuum. Scan the following table and mark the appropriate boxes for your level and relevance for each CQ essential.

Note: You will find invitations to ask your accountability partner to join in the conversation in various chapters. Now might be a good time to connect with your partner about where you are and he or she is in the CQ process.

Back to the proficiency continuum, here are descriptions for each level:

- **NOVICE.** I have a basic understanding of the concept and apply it effectively in some situations.
- **INTERMEDIATE.** I have opportunities to learn about the concept and apply it more effectively in most routine work situations.
- **MASTERY.** I proactively study the concept, have personalized strategies to apply it in almost all circumstances, and am able to mentor and teach others in this area.

10 ESSENTIAL CQ SKILLS	DESCRIPTION	WHERE I AM I NOW *Mark each box with N (novice), I (intermediate), or M (mastery).*	CURRENT RELEVANCE *Mark each box with SR (somewhat relevant), VR (very relevant), or P (current priority)*
CQ1: Clear, consistent communication	The test is whether your *message* is *understood* by the receiver *in the way you intended it.* When the *two align,* there is *clear communication.*		
CQ2: Balancing empathy	The *intersection of empathy and CQ,* properly executed, can be a *solid strategy* to *bring your best* to work and *maximize productivity for yourself and others.*		
CQ3: Proactive listening	*Proactive listening* is much more than processing words. It is about *ensuring someone* is *heard all the way* through.		
CQ4: Expanding safe spaces	All employees have the *right to feel* that they're *emotionally, physically, and psychologically safe at work.* Can *all workplaces* be *safe spaces?*		
CQ5: Communicating with challenging people	Is it *the person* or the *behavior* that *you perceive as challenging?* There is *almost always common ground* if we're open to finding it.		
CQ6: Receiving and giving ongoing feedback	*Feedback,* delivered constructively and with strengths in mind, is designed to *improve future actions* and performance. And *it's everywhere*—it's our choice to see and receive it!		
CQ7: Got questions?	*Ask questions* that the *other person* will *want to answer.* The *answers you receive* depend on the *questions you ask.*		

(continued on next page)

10 ESSENTIAL CQ SKILLS	DESCRIPTION	WHERE I AM I NOW Mark each box with N (novice), I (intermediate), or M (mastery).	CURRENT RELEVANCE Mark each box with SR (somewhat relevant), VR (very relevant), or P (current priority)
CQ8: Crystallizing non-verbal communication	When your *words and non-verbal signals align,* your *CQ crystallizes* and *builds trust and confidence* in you and your message.		
CQ9: Connecting through virtual communication	*Communication is the number one skill* employees need to *succeed in the virtual or hybrid* worlds of work. What's the second? Adaptability.		
CQ10: Earning trust	As you *earn and grant trust,* the *dividends far exceed the investment.*		

Now that you have completed the table, answer these questions:

Which areas emerged as *priorities for you now* in terms of your level of proficiency and current relevancy?

_____

_____

_____

A part of CQ is positioning for future success. Which areas do you believe may be key *in the future* (e.g., the next one to three months or a longer time frame)?

_____

_____

_____

Learning more about these areas and applying strategies is part of being your best at work and in life. Although each CQ is a stand-alone segment, each also intersects with others that will be relevant. For example, if a focus is receiving and giving feedback, you will at least want to tune into balancing empathy, got questions, and non-verbal communication.

As you move through the CQ 10, are there essentials that would benefit a colleague or your accountability partner? Tuning into, and sharing, this information is part of bringing your best to work. Completing and then reviewing the table will help to set you up for success with the next steps.

COLLEAGUE	CQ 10 AREA(S) OF POTENTIAL INTEREST

Are you ready for the next stage of your journey toward Communication Intelligence mastery?

WHAT'S NEXT?

In the next chapter on CQ1, you'll hear from focus group members who gathered to talk about clear and consistent communication.

CQ1: CLEAR, CONSISTENT COMMUNICATION

*The measure is whether the message that you intend
to send is the same one that is understood by the receiver.
When the two align, there is clear communication.*

I facilitated a focus group the other day on the topic of clear, consistent communication. Sitting around the table were 10 talented professionals from a variety of sectors and with varying communication strengths. The majority had extrovert as a primary strength. As well, there were more than a few dominants, a conformist/introvert, and a patient/non-dominant. I was the only conformist/impatient in the room (which is not unusual). I adapted my natural tendency and sat back, somewhat patiently, to listen to the conversation. Yes, there was a time when I did not have a grasp on how to do this. Today I never facilitate a meeting without viewing the group's Forté Team Pulse Report and planning my adapting style and messaging accordingly.

After introducing the topic of clear, consistent communication, I asked if any of the group members had an example from their work experience. You could have heard a pin drop . . . for a millisecond.

The extroverts, of course, were the first to weigh in. There was a barrage of examples—however, not of the positive kind. They were of miscommunication, lack of clarity, and communication derailers. Here's a taste of what was on the topic menu:

- **THOSE (SOMETIMES) DARNED EMAILS!** Studies show that professionals spend more than half their workweek dealing with written communication, with emails high on the list. This was the first topic that the group identified. The extroverts were very verbal and clear, and "If it takes more than two emails, please call me!" They offered the following suggestions: "Please keep them short." "Don't copy me when it's not necessary." "Get to the point and use bullets." And "Do they even open the emails that I send?"

- **NONSTOP TALKERS.** Another extrovert example was not getting a chance to chime in. "There was a very intelligent partner who was giving a presentation and just kept talking without taking a breath or letting anyone ask a question. I couldn't tell if she was nervous or oblivious as to her audience. It was exhausting," offered an extrovert.

  "I know what you mean. I had an initial meeting with a prospect the other day, and he talked for more than four hours. My boss and I were done after the first 30 minutes," added a dominant, preferring to-the-point communications.

- **VIRTUAL CHALLENGES.** There was agreement that virtual and hybrid workspaces present their own set of CQ challenges. Specifically, "I prefer it one-on-one," offered the conformist/introvert. There was no consensus on whether there should be a set of rules for virtual—the non-conformists, of course, weren't as comfortable with structure as the conformists.

- **CHOICE OF MEDIUM—WRITTEN, IN PERSON, VIRTUAL, OR HYBRID?** The ambivert felt: "There's a time for virtual and a time for face-to-face. That's 2D and 3D. Two-dimensional is in a virtual encounter when there's more limited perception. And three-dimensional is when there's in-person communication and more robust interaction."

An extrovert offered: "I had a boss whose office was 20 feet away from mine. She sent me an email and then walked down the hall to see if I received it."

The extrovert who was also patient shared: "It's more challenging to build a long-term relationship with a client on video—when they're in another country, you don't have a choice. If this focus group conversation were virtual, we wouldn't have the same connection."

- **ASSUMPTIONS.** The patient said: "It's frustrating when someone makes assumptions about what I know or how I think. In business, we shouldn't assume. Isn't the goal usually to create a meeting of the minds?"

  In response, the dominant said: "How often does that actually happen? Instead, it seems there's all of this wasted time because somebody assumed. And then you leave a meeting thinking, 'I don't know what they mean or what they want me to do.'"

- **TEACHERS RULE.** Although all the professions represented in the room owned up to having communication challenges, the three current or past teachers won the prize. Collectively, they said: "You have to work constantly at clear, consistent communication when there are 30 sets of young eyes looking at you. You need to reach each of them in a different way. Every minute of every workday, regardless of external circumstances." Enough said.

- **GET TO THE POINT! IT'S ABOUT TIME AND RESPECT.** An area of consensus was that when someone communicates in a clear and concise manner, it sends a signal of respect. A dominant/impatient added: "We only have so much time, and when someone burdens me with having to wade through lengthy emails, documents without bullets or an executive summary, or an oratory that never gets to the point, it's a waste of my time. And theirs. Please, show some respect and tell me what you want me to know or do—clearly, directly, and concisely."

What about you? Do you have examples of when less than effective communication has derailed or caused disruption to work flow or the work environment? The big question is, does it happen often, and if so, what can be done about it? You'll find the answer to this throughout the book!

HOW ABOUT CLEAR COMMUNICATION?

The fact that the focus group started with examples of communication derailers initiated by *others* is not unusual. What about when you are the initiator instead of the receiver?

This has probably happened to you where you think your idea through and present it to others. But somehow, what you thought was crystal clear isn't received as such, and the results are less than expected. This is incredibly frustrating, and it's so worth the effort to get this right. The measure is whether the message that you intend to send is the same message that is understood by the receiver. When the two align, there is clear communication. The good news is that clear, consistent communication can be learned.

Based on almost five decades of my research into CQ interactions, it is evident that a clear message has two key elements: our roles as initiators and listeners:

- *As initiators,* each of us is responsible for bringing as much clarity as possible to communication, whether it be verbal, non-verbal, written, or visual.
- *As listeners,* each of us needs to develop and use our *proactive listening skills* to ultimately determine how we perceive what we have been presented.

Both initiating and listening are skills that, more often than not, we learn through real-life experiences of what has worked and what hasn't. To succeed in life, we definitely want to rack up more successes as our communication with others evolves. Often, the reality is although the individual had worked hard to achieve clarity of the message, it was misperceived by the recipient. How can we minimize the likelihood of miscommunication? There is a way!

It comes down to perception. The listener's perception is his or her reality. This is true whether that reality be an experience, a message, a background, a methodology, a native language in a global world, or a state of mind.

WHERE ARE YOU NOW?

What is your current level when it comes to clear, consistent communication?

LEVEL	DESCRIPTORS	WHERE I AM NOW
Novice	I primarily practice one-way communication. I rarely adapt my message based on the receiver.	
Intermediate	I tend to listen as much as I speak. I like to check that the receiver understands my message.	
Proficient—mastery	I recognize I am primarily responsible for the intent of my message being understood. I proactively work to ensure my intended message is aligned with the receiver's understanding.	

In this chapter you will:

- Hear from focus group members about the *impact* (and lack) *of clear, consistent communication at work.*
- Consider *12 communication strategies* to enhance clear, consistent communication.
- Prioritize the 12 strategies in terms of your *stronger abilities and development opportunities.*

12 COMMUNICATION STRATEGIES

Here are a dozen strategies that can add up to clearer, more consistent communication. They are based on dozens of focus groups and hundreds of thousands of interactions investigating Communication Intelligence. After each description is an action tip. As you consider each, note those that you believe are already strong abilities and those that you could improve through attention and intention.

> Consider inviting your accountability partner to work through your priority items with you—and offer the same opportunity to your partner.

This chapter and these enhancers set the stage for the rest of the 10 CQ essentials. In the chapters ahead, you will find references and deeper insights about them. You will find that some of the 12 enhancers have a lighter treatment here than others. Consider this a lightning round with additional information planted through the chapters ahead.

1. **ACCEPT YOUR RESPONSIBILITY.** As noted above, when you initiate a communication, it is primarily your responsibility for the message to be heard and interpreted as you intend it. Yes, the listener has a role to play and ideally will be an active listener and participate constructively. And it is true that both parties are voluntarily participating in the conversation. However, this is not an equal partnership in terms of who is responsible for leading and steering the conversation to the initiator's intended outcome.

   The initiator has the primary role. No one else has invested the thought and time that you have. Learn your audience in advance, as best you can; this definitely puts the first step in place. It's about them, not you.

CQ ACTION TIP. In a next conversation, assume the primary role for ensuring the message is understood as intended. The tips below will help you achieve this goal.

2. **APPLY YOUR COMMUNICATION STRENGTHS AND ADAPT YOUR BEHAVIOR.** In our focus group, the introverts waited for a while before inserting themselves into the conversation. And they were successful. The extroverts paused long enough to listen and ask relevant questions.

    CQ ACTION TIP. Refer to your CQ strengths and your natural tendencies, and adapt based on the participants, the situation, and the environment.

3. **KNOW YOUR AUDIENCE.** This is near the top of the list for most people when it comes to clear communication. Knowing your audience means being aware of people's communication strengths—their tendencies and preferences. It means considering their background, experiences, position, and state of mind in framing your communication. You can find out what you need to by doing prior research (almost everyone is present in the Google-sphere—e.g., LinkedIn) or asking questions at the beginning of an interaction.

    CQ ACTION TIP. Do your research to learn about the participant(s) or audience before interacting.

4. **DEFINE YOUR PURPOSE.** On a broad level, there generally are four purposes for communication:
   - To inform or share information, including responding to a request or query
   - To collect or gather information
   - To solve a problem or brainstorm about new ideas
   - To express feelings or promote social interaction

   The key is to be clear, first with yourself and then through your communication with others, about the purpose.

CQ ACTION TIP. What are your upcoming communication opportunities today? What is the purpose of each? It is helpful to write them down. Give it a try.

COMMUNICATION OPPORTUNITY	PURPOSE

5. **USE SHARED LANGUAGE (VERSUS TECHNICAL JARGON, ACRONYMS).** This ties to the earlier point about making assumptions about your audience—that is, you shouldn't assume that your choice of words will be interpreted by others in the way you understand them. This should also be a wake-up call for those at the novice level of CQ. For example, those who believe that using big words and talking above others' heads will make others see them, somehow, as more important or powerful. It's not about *you*; it's about your intended message and the receiver. Watch jargon, technical language, cultural references, inappropriate humor, and other elements that might be misunderstood or not understood by those in the room.

   Choose language that is shared by all those involved— language that is relatable, familiar, and accessible. This will help build relationships (versus confusion or alienation).

   CQ ACTION TIP. Invest the time to review that email, memo, or presentation. Are there word choices or references that could be unclear, misunderstood, or even offensive? Are you choosing shared language for your audience?

6. **FOCUS THE MESSAGE.** What is the key message you want to convey? *Focus in* to communicate it in the clearest and most concise manner. Here's an example of a less than clear spoken message (word count: 81):

   "I'm not sure we really have a choice here. I mean, the contract needs to be sent to the client on Friday, and

I don't think it will be ready by then. Unless, of course, we can get someone in legal to peel away and review it ahead of schedule. They're always so busy down there. I guess we should let the client know there might be a delay. I know they won't be happy, but do we have a choice?"

The above message is fragmented, and the words are rambling. It's as though the speaker is thinking out loud without considering the receptivity of the audience. If I'm listening, I'd be confused and unclear about what the initiator is asking.

The message below is shorter and more to the point (word count: 42):

"The contract is due Friday. Here are our action steps. Please contact Marion in legal—can she have the contract reviewed by Thursday? If not, identify a specific day and time. I'll contact the client and confirm or set a new deadline."

As the listener, I'm clear through this communication what is being asked of me. I have more confidence that the speaker knows what should be done and am motivated to take action.

Here's the same shorter message as it might appear clearly in an email:

"The *contract* is *due Friday*. Here are our action steps:
- Please *contact Marion in legal*—can she have the contract *reviewed by Thursday?*
- If not, *identify a specific day and time.*
- *I'll contact the client and confirm or set a new deadline.*"

Shorter and more direct sentences are easier to understand. The more focused you are on the key message, the more likely the recipient will comprehend your intended meaning. Start with what you want people to know or what you want them to do.

In written communication, formatting can be friendly—bullets, **bolding**, <u>underlining</u>, *italics*, shorter paragraphs, tables. Proper application can allow the readers to skim across the words and grasp your primary points. The readers can then return and dig for deeper understanding, if they are so inclined.

Simpler is clearer. Succinct is elegant. Uncomplicated is the mark of a professional.

> **CQ ACTION TIP.** Over the next week, make it a priority to focus on key points in your messaging. This may mean reviewing emails and written documents and cutting out unnecessary language. Consider having a conversation with your accountability partner during which you both focus on main messages—while being relatable.

7. **BE A PROACTIVE LISTENER.** This also is an item that comes out at the top of most communication tip lists. (Chapter 10 is devoted to proactive listening.) Dr. Ralph Nichols, also known as the father of the "field of listening," said that "the most basic of all human needs is the need to understand and be understood. The best way to understand people is to listen to them." There's a distinction between being a passive listener—when your mind is racing ahead with an answer or floating off to what's next on the day's agenda or this evening's leisure activity—and being a proactive listener, which is when you are fully present, focused on the communication, and working to interpret the message as intended. When you initiate a conversation, it is important that you are alert to non-verbal and verbal cues from your audience to decipher whether you are being truly heard.

> **CQ ACTION TIP.** A good rule is to invest at least as much time listening as talking in any interaction. Over the next few days, turn down your speaking volume and ramp up your proactive listening.

8. **ASK QUESTIONS/CHECK FOR UNDERSTANDING.** There's also a chapter on asking effective questions later in the book (see Chapter 14) since it's at the top of the CQ tips list for most professionals. The key point here is, how will you know if the listener has understood your intended message? If you are the initiator, and particularly if the communication is important (e.g., a direction related to accomplishing a business outcome or safety), a good practice is to ask a question inviting your listeners to repeat what you said in their own words (instead of accepting a "Yes, I understand" or a head nod).

    CQ ACTION TIP. If you are the recipient or listener and want to be sure you got the message or are unclear, you can try saying:
    - "Let me be sure I understand what you are saying..."
    - "Help me understand exactly what that means to you..."
    - "I want to be sure I am interpreting you correctly..."
    - "What I hear you saying is... —does that make sense?
    - "I want to make sure we're on the same page..."

9. **MIND NON-VERBAL COMMUNICATION.** This is another CQ enhancer that has a dedicated chapter ahead (Chapter 15). The main point is that the majority of how our communication is perceived is based on non-verbal cues instead of actual words. This is primarily composed of body language, facial expressions, and tone of voice.

    CQ ACTION TIP. The first step is to be aware of your non-verbal communication and its impact on your ability to communicate clearly. If this is one of your priority enhancers, review Chapter 15, "CQ8: Crystallizing Non-Verbal Communication."

10. **USE PAUSES VERSUS (UM, YOU KNOW) FILLERS.** Have you ever listened to a presentation—maybe a TED Talk or at a conference—and it's hard to focus on the message because every few words there is just, kind of, you know, like—a filler? It even, um, can really happen, in like plain, um, everyday conversation, right?

    Research shows that speakers who use fewer fillers are perceived as more confident than those who use more. And it can be downright, um, annoying, can't it, like you know?

Most people have habitual fillers. Do you know yours? Like most aspects of communication, this is where awareness comes in. Record yourself talking. Watch yourself in the mirror. Ask your accountability partner or good friend to provide you with constructive feedback.

You can train yourself to use fewer fillers and punch up your key points with pauses:

- First, start being more aware of when you use fillers. At first, you probably will be aware *after* you have said them. A tip here is to speak a bit more slowly. *Note:* As you do this, you will likely become more aware of others' use of fillers.
- As your awareness grows, you will likely become aware of fillers *while* you are saying them.
- Soon you will be aware *before* you say them.
- Then use pauses (instead of fillers). Pausing at key points helps display confidence (versus fillers, which undermine the listener's confidence). Pauses also help to emphasize key points. For example:
  - *Fillers:* Um, so, a key to—you know—clear communication is to kind of avoid fillers when you are talking. So a good way to do that is to, um, be aware of when you're using them, right?
  - *Pauses:* A key to clear communication *(shorter pause)* is to avoid fillers. *(longer pause)* A good way to do that *(shorter pause)* is to be aware of when you're using them.

  CQ ACTION TIP. Over the next week, use the above strategies to (1) identify your filler habits and (2) replace them with pauses.

Ask your accountability partner to record a short conversation with you at the beginning and the end of the week. Do you notice a difference?

11. **KEEP IT POSITIVE.** As you've probably gathered by now, this is one of my favorite topics, and I've included it in training for decades. Positivity is contagious. Whether you choose to turn a phrase in an upbeat or negative direction can make or break someone's day. It starts with your attitude and then is translated through your verbal and non-verbal communication.

    For the purposes of clear, consistent communication, one guideline is to skew your body language, tone of voice, and eye contact toward the positive—for example, smile authentically; maintain appropriate eye contact; laugh! Another guideline is to choose positive phrases over negative ones in written and verbal communication. Here are some ideas.

MORE NEGATIVE	MORE POSITIVE
Just . . . , Sorry . . .	Don't use "just" or "sorry" unless there is a specific justification and meaning.
But . . .	In most cases, you can replace "but" with "and" or "however."
I don't . . . , I can't . . .	I am not able to at the moment . . .
Never . . .	Not yet . . .
If only . . .	When or if this happens, . . .
Don't ever . . .	Instead of . . .

A note on humor: What's the value of humor in CQ? You can't overestimate the amount that appropriate humor can add to the work environment. Humor empowers relationships; it eases tension; it invites others to listen to you more. Humor can make you and your message memorable. You can be someone's hero when you use appropriate humor to make the workspace a fun and enjoyable place to be! We can all use an invitation to lighten up. Why not be the one to make 'em laugh?

CQ ACTION TIP. You have a choice—positive or negative. Choose positive!

12. **PRACTICE CQ INTEGRITY.** People of integrity do the right thing for the right reason at the right time. And they do what they say they are going to and when. Dr. Tony Simons of Cornell University wrote *The Integrity Dividend: Leading by the Power of Your Word*, which is a book that covers research he conducted into the impact of integrity at work. He found that when managers followed up on their commitments to team members, productivity increased by almost 20 percent. *Consistency is key to integrity.* When you communicate that you are going to take an action—do it. If there is a legitimate reason that you cannot keep a commitment, let the other party know as soon as possible and reschedule, and provide a specific day and time.

   CQ ACTION TIP. For most people, it promotes integrity when you make fewer commitments, are more aware of them, and make it a priority to track and keep them.

ON THE ROAD TO CQ MASTERY— CLEAR, CONSISTENT COMMUNICATION

There's a lot to digest here. All the proficient communicators I know have committed to a lifelong journey toward CQ mastery. No matter where you are in your journey, you can start this way:

- *Identify*:
    - The top one to two areas where you already have strong abilities
    - And one development opportunity
- *Review* the related CQ action tips.
- *Practice them for one week.* Then assess and repeat. Or identify additional enhancers.

CQ ENHANCER	ONE TO TWO STRENGTHS	ONE DEVELOPMENT OPPORTUNITY	WEEK 1	WEEK 2	WEEK 3
Accept your responsibility.					
Apply your communication strength and adapt your behavior.					
Know your audience.					
Define your purpose.					
Use shared language.					
Focus the message.					
Be a proactive listener.					
Ask questions/check for understanding.					
Mind non-verbal communication.					
Use pauses versus (um, you know) fillers.					
Keep it positive.					
Practice CQ integrity.					

WHAT'S NEXT?

Did you know that empathy is tied to harmonious relationships and positive business outcomes? Find out more in the next chapter on balancing empathy.

CQ2: BALANCING EMPATHY

The intersection of empathy and CQ
leads to harmonious relationships.

NBC News recently ran a story about Randy, who was asked to officiate at the wedding of his sister-in-law, Jamie, and her husband-to-be, Brian. He learned that the couple had invited Brian's niece, an adorable two-year-old girl named Riley, to be the flower girl in the ceremony. He was inspired (as is everyone who meets her) by the joyful nature that emanates from this little girl. He also learned that Riley was born deaf, has cochlear implants, and has been learning American Sign Language (ASL).

Randy imagined what it would be like to be in Riley's shoes, walking down the aisle and then not being able to hear what was being said at the altar. He had an idea. Over many weeks, he secretly dedicated time and energy to learn ASL in order to communicate the vows. He was determined that everyone, especially little Riley, would feel included on this special day. Riley's parents were overwhelmed, and others in attendance were moved and inspired, when Randy spoke and signed. He set an example of empathy and inclusion that they will never forget.

I believe that the story of Randy and Riley is a prime illustration of what can happen when empathy and CQ intersect. As Randy states, "It's become a much bigger message about the little things we can do in our everyday lives to make people feel welcome and seen and heard."

WHERE ARE YOU NOW?

It's time for the novice to mastery question. In the table that follows, indicate your level of proficiency in terms of empathy.

LEVEL	BEHAVIORS	WHERE I AM NOW
Novice	I can confuse empathy with sympathy. I'm not sure how it translates into productivity.	
Intermediate	I understand empathy is important for constructive relationships with colleagues and clients. I try to see things from others' perspectives.	
Mastery	I actively seek to understand the thoughts and emotions of others and to adapt my behavior from their perspective. I can describe the positive impact empathy has on relationships and business outcomes.	

In this chapter you will:

- Gain clarity on *what empathy is* and how it *builds respect and rapport* to strengthen relationships.
- Explore *how communication strengths* can positively impact the *application of empathy*.
- Identify *actions you can take* to promote *empathy* in communicating with colleagues and clients.

WHAT IS EMPATHY?

What if you couldn't wait to get to work each day? What if this was a space where you felt understood, supported, and encouraged by colleagues and managers? What if this is where you are happy and engaged and enjoy being your best self? And this is where all your colleagues felt the same. That's where empathy comes in.

Empathy is the ability to relate to and communicate based on the emotions, thinking, and experiences of others. There is a reason it has become a popular topic in a work context. A number of research studies demonstrate a correlation between higher levels of empathy and stronger communication, more harmonious relationships, increased customer loyalty, and other better business outcomes.

The benefits of empathy at work include the following:

- **IMPROVES COMMUNICATION.** Applying empathy helps you adapt communication in interactions with colleagues and clients based on *their* thoughts, feelings, and experiences. Coming up, there is more specific information about how communication strengths apply to empathy in practice.
- **PREVENTS MISCOMMUNICATION AND PROMOTES CONFLICT RESOLUTION.** When you seek to communicate with the understanding of another's perspective, you can prevent miscommunication and resolve conflicts in a healthy manner.
- **ENCOURAGES RESPECT, RAPPORT, AND MORE HARMONIOUS RELATIONSHIPS.** When you are a team member who empathizes with your colleagues, they feel more at ease and like being around you. Team members with a goal of understanding each other act to support each other, especially when there are challenges.
- **MOTIVATES INDIVIDUALS EFFECTIVELY.** When leaders understand the thoughts and needs of those on their team, they are able to delegate in ways that will motivate, inspire, and promote productivity. When a performer starts to become disengaged at work, empathetic colleagues are more supportive because they are attuned to the symptoms of burnout.
- **BOOSTS SOLUTIONS THINKING.** When you are able to think and feel in terms of what your clients (internal or external) desire— or, better yet, *anticipate their needs before they realize them*—you are much closer to tailoring a solution that will meet their needs.

- **PROMOTES INNOVATION AND CREATIVITY.** Related to solutions thinking, empathy allows you to have insights beyond words. Microsoft CEO Satya Nadella said that "if I look at the most successful products we have ever created, it comes with that ability to meet the unmet, unarticulated needs of customers." We are so many times so close to the needs of others, we do not see them. This is especially true in business. Adopt a "listen between the lines" approach with your customers, clients, patients, or those you serve. This is a key element of CQ.

- **EARNS CUSTOMER LOYALTY.** When you apply an empathy strategy throughout a customer experience (e.g., designing a product, providing a service), you are positioned to outpace the competition in serving the customer. This leads to customer loyalty and potential referrals.

- **RATES HIGHER IN TERMS OF EMPATHY ROI (RETURN ON INVESTMENT).** The Empathy Index was developed by a research and consulting firm called The Empathy Business. The survey was designed to answer the question: "Which companies are successfully creating empathetic cultures? These are the companies that retain the best people, create environments where diverse teams thrive, and ultimately reap the greatest financial rewards." The researchers noted that businesses named at the top of the index earn 50 percent more per employee than those lower on the list. The value of those at the top also increased twice *as fast* as those further down.

However, there is confusion about how empathy actually plays out in the workplace. Your capacity for, and experience with, empathy may vary based on communication strengths, your occupational sector, and your role. It's safe to say that empathy is not a one-size-fits-all proposition.

CLARIFYING EMPATHY

There is general agreement that empathy has value at work. There also is a majority view that organizations could improve in this area. According to a study by the consulting firm Emtrain, 86 percent of employees strongly agree that empathy is important as a conversation skill in the workplace. However, less than half that number strongly agree that they perceive empathy in how colleagues communicate. The study also concludes that less than one-third (31 percent) of employees say that managers show empathy toward direct reports.

A factor contributing to the confusion is that empathy can mean different things to different people. It can be helpful to clarify the distinction between sympathy and empathy, as the two terms have been used interchangeably. The term "sympathy" is when you feel bad or sad for what people are going through. You may pity them without any real understanding of what they are experiencing or feeling. "Empathy," as noted above, refers to having the interest and capacity to relate to others through identifying with their thoughts, emotions, and experiences. If you become proficient at this, a whole new world opens up. And it has been there all along! True leaders have this in their playbook!

THE THREE EMPATHY CATEGORIES

Daniel Goleman is the author and psychologist known for his work with emotional intelligence. He offers a way to consider empathy in terms of three categories—cognitive, emotional, and compassionate. The following table breaks down what this can mean in a work context.

CATEGORY	DESCRIPTION	PROS	CONSIDERATIONS
Cognitive	**Intellect:** Knowing (versus feeling) how another might feel. This primarily involves thoughts at an intellectual level or understanding.	This behavior is an advantage when some emotional distance may be an asset. One example would be an HR person who has to dismiss a team of employees. Another example would be a negotiator who has to draw a hard line to achieve an outcome.	The person demonstrating cognitive empathy can be viewed as detached or disconnected from others. In situations where interacting based on another's feelings is valued, this behavior can be a disadvantage.
Emotional	**Intellect and emotion:** This is when there is a physical connection with another's emotions. You feel the person's emotions as if those emotions were your own. For example, if someone is hurting, that person's pain is yours. If someone is happy, that person's joy is yours.	Connecting at an emotional level can create a solid and intimate bond with another. It can be helpful in occupations that benefit from building close and deep relationships.	This level of empathy could be viewed as inappropriate by some or in some circumstances. For example, if you are leading a team in a complex and time-sensitive situation where objectivity is required, being emotionally involved with someone can distract. This may also lead to being overly involved in others' personal problems at work.
Compassionate	**Intellect, emotion, and action:** Compassionate empathy is a balance between cognitive and emotional empathy. This is when you understand and feel another's experience, and then respond (often spontaneously) appropriately and with compassion.	This is a good balance in most situations. You understand intellectually and don't get overwhelmed by others' emotions. For example, you listen when someone is hurting or wants to share good news. You step in to help when someone is stressed and needs a break.	Can you think of a time when you've been on the receiving end of compassionate empathy? It can be an appropriate basis for communication in many, if not most, situations.

The three categories of empathy—cognitive, emotional, and compassionate—underscore that there is a need to find a balance in CQ that is a good fit for the giver, receiver, and situation.

CAN EMPATHY INFLUENCE JUDGMENT?

There are those who challenge the value of empathy and cite its potential impact to interfere with our judgment and objectivity. If we are completely invested in someone else to the point we are immersed in the other person's thoughts and feelings (e.g., emotional empathy), can we represent a team's or organization's interests? As examples:

- Consider a teacher who is so empathetic to a student whose "dog ate the homework" that she's unable to fairly respond to other students in the class who need attention or to uphold a school's policies.
- Would you want an emergency room nurse to be so emotionally drawn into the pain that those in her care are feeling, that she suffers stress and the risk of burnout?
- What about a soldier in battle, an airplane pilot in an emergency situation, or a firefighter working to control a fire?

There are cases when one needs to have the self-awareness and skills to balance extreme empathy with the needs of a job or situation.

COMMUNICATION STRENGTHS AND EMPATHY

A way to be ahead of the curve in applying empathy at work is to review communication strengths and their potential impact on interactions. The items below offer suggestions for how you can extend empathy to others:

DOMINANCE

Tendency. View every interaction from a person as a problem to be solved.

Empathy. Practice seeing the person behind the problem and listening between the lines.

NON-DOMINANCE

Tendency. Overshare or take on other people's problems as your own.

Empathy. Practice situational awareness and setting boundaries.

EXTROVERSION

Tendency. Enjoy lively conversation and being the center of attention.

Empathy. Practice pausing and allowing for others' input and response.

INTROVERSION

Tendency. Not show much facial expression or engaging body language.

Empathy. Practice offering "encouraging cues" to let the other party know you are present and engaged.

AMBIVERSION

Tendency. Be regarded as moody because you easily move between extroversion and introversion.

Empathy. Practice signaling when you don't have the bandwidth for an interaction and then scheduling a time when you can give your full attention.

PATIENCE

Tendency. When pressured to respond, will say what you think the other person wants to hear just to get that person "out of your face."

Empathy. Practice asking for time to think about the problem and offer a time to get back to the person.

IMPATIENCE

Tendency. Make assumptions and jump to conclusions.

Empathy. Practice resisting the urge to interrupt, and instead listen to the end; use the power of the pause before responding to what's being said.

CONFORMITY

Tendency. Ask many questions as a means of understanding and buy-in.

Empathy. Practice repeating back what your understanding is first before jumping in with "21 questions."

NON-CONFORMITY

Tendency. Explore all the ways to improve/expand on someone's idea.

Empathy. Practice affirming the other person first, and ask if he or she is seeking feedback or just looking for a sounding board.

ON THE ROAD TO CQ MASTERY—BALANCING EMPATHY

Are you ready to apply more intentional empathy at work and in life? Consider the following table and situations you have coming up over the next few days. For example:

- Maybe you will be facilitating a team meeting and have the opportunity to read the primary strengths in the room and adapt your approach for each individual.
- Perhaps you have an upcoming one-on-one session with your boss and you are interested in applying empathy to help manage up.
- Is there a client kickoff meeting where you can integrate empathy into your discovery phase to uncover needs and wants the people

in your audience may not be aware of yet? With whom, where, and how will you balance empathy?

DATE	COLLEAGUE	COLLEAGUE'S PRIMARY STRENGTH	SITUATION	ACTIONS I'LL APPLY	RESULTS

WHAT'S NEXT?

CQ3 is proactive listening, which is related to balancing empathy and other CQ essentials. It's much more than processing words. It's about ensuring someone is heard all the way through.

CHAPTER
10

CQ3: PROACTIVE LISTENING

The best communicator is the best listener.

It was not just any Sunday afternoon; it was a Sunday in May on the last day of a major golf championship with the famed Wanamaker Trophy on the line. At the start of the day, there was a player who was seven shots back. The bookmakers didn't give him good odds of taking a run at what would have been the second major win of his career. His less than stellar play on Saturday (he'd shot a 4 over 74) weighed heavily on his mind as familiar negative thoughts took hold. The player recalled, "I just needed to let some steam out. I didn't need to bring my frustration and anger home with me. I didn't need to leave the golf course in a negative frame of mind."

You may be familiar with the role that caddies play in the game of golf. These under-the-radar stars are tasked primarily with carrying their players' clubs as well as offering advice and moral support, as appropriate.

After the round of 74 on Saturday, this caddie had a mission—to ensure that his golfer got the message loud and clear that he should stay positive and that he could win. He knew what to say, he knew how to manage the message, and he knew his player. The challenge was, would the man set to play on the course listen to the man on the bag? After all, "being an effective listener" isn't in the job description of a professional golfer. As the player recalls, "He was just like, 'Dude, you've got to stop being so hard on yourself. You're in contention every single week we're playing.'" The meaning, intent, and tone of the caddie's message got through and inspired the golfer to listen and change his attitude and his outcome.

At the end of the tournament on Sunday, it was the pro, Justin Thomas, standing in the winner's circle of the PGA Championship with his caddy, Jim "Bones" Mackay, standing nearby. Justin went on to say, "I'm fully confident in saying that I wouldn't be standing here if he didn't give me that— wasn't necessarily a speech, but a talk, if you will." And Justin wouldn't be holding the Wanamaker Trophy if he didn't make the choice that Saturday afternoon to be a champion listener.

Listening is Communication Intelligence. Not listening, to be frank, demonstrates a lack of CQ. Something that is easily overlooked is that being effective communicators requires us to be proactive listeners. In fact, the best communicator is the best listener. We tend to take listening for granted, and most have not given it the deep thought it deserves.

Let's dig in.

WHERE ARE YOU NOW?

First, where are you today regarding listening—novice, intermediate, or mastery?

CQ LEVEL	DESCRIPTORS	WHERE I AM NOW
Novice	I haven't really thought about listening. I can distinguish between hearing someone and listening to someone.	
Intermediate	I am aware of the impact of listening and not listening. I have tried to listen, and it's not always easy. I have learned more about listening through reading, a class, or a conversation with others.	
Mastery	I understand why listening is an essential CQ skill that you can evolve. I can describe the impact of listening (and not listening) at work. I have specific actions that I take based on my CQ strengths, and those of others, to improve listening.	

In this chapter, you will:

- Understand the *value of proactive listening*.
- Identify *barriers to effective listening*.
- Determine *steps for CQ listening* that are most relevant for you today and in the future.

THE VALUE OF LISTENING

You've likely heard about active listening skills, which include choosing a quiet, distraction-free environment, asking one question at a time, not jumping to conclusions or solutions, and summarizing back to the person what you've heard. Active listening generally concerns itself with the messages on the surface level. Proactive listening is much more than processing words. It's about being prepared to listen and ensuring people are heard all the way through. It is acknowledging that their communicating is an essential part of being human. And ignoring what people are saying is among the biggest personal insults you can inflict on others. It is also extremely damaging to a work environment. Shortly thereafter, those people will not be listening to you, and that will begin a downward spiral.

Like other aspects of Communication Intelligence, proactive listening builds relationships. It is a way people learn and grow together. It promotes civility in the workspace. When there is strong listening, a group of individuals evolve into an effective team. Listening also can prevent and resolve conflicts. Low-quality listening is associated with a lack of interest in sharing honest views ("If they don't care, why should I bother?") and negative business outcomes. Research also shows that listening promotes productivity, as it increases understanding and facilitates the flow of information. It is how individuals gain the knowledge they need to perform well.

The impact of the failure to listen at work can be dramatic, even life-threatening in cases when communication about a safety issue isn't listened to. Listening derailers can include distracted listening, superficial listening, and a lack of follow-up action. There are ways to counter or overcome the impact of derailers. A prime example is making colleagues feel valued through listening to them all the way through.

FEELING VALUED

A major outcome that distinguishes listening from other aspects of communication is that it can lead to people feeling appreciated at work. When, as a listener, you are fully and intentionally present, the speaker knows that you take what he or she is saying seriously.

Mister Rogers' Neighborhood of Value

Fred Rogers was the host, writer, and producer of *Mister Rogers' Neighborhood*, the iconic PBS show for children of all ages that ran on public television for more than 30 years. A primary reason for Mister Rogers' popularity and longevity was that he had that ability to make everyone in his orbit feel special and valued. Whoever he was listening to was the entire focus and the most important thing in his life at that moment. His secret? He was an exceptionally proactive and attentive listener. He took time to slow down and never judge the speaker or have preconceived assumptions. The character, Mister Rogers, understood that listening is not just about receiving information; it is about emotions and feelings. The writer and producer Fred Rogers must have known that the way people listen is influenced by their communication strengths, and we can adapt to make sure everyone feels heard.

TWO CONTRASTING MEETINGS

Here are two scenarios of how listening and communication strengths can play out in the workplace. Please note in the scenarios that the outcome is not just dependent on the choices made by the listener—the presenter of the message also takes actions, and responsibility, for setting up a receptive situation.

Meeting Scenario 1

This scenario features Joshua (whose primary strength is patience) and Trisha (whose primary strength is dominance).

SITUATION. Joshua has been tasked with finding a way to help his team store information in a more efficient and user-friendly way. He has invested overtime researching a solution and believes he has a solid approach. It may not be perfect, but he's excited to run it by Trisha, the IT lead. He sent a pretty vague and lengthy email asking for a meeting that Trisha barely skimmed before setting a date and time.

ACTION. Trisha, the IT lead, and Joshua show up for the meeting on time and exchange pleasantries. Now it's Joshua's turn to shine; he's thinking this is going to be big!

COMMUNICATION INTELLIGENCE

Joshua tries to catch Trisha's eye, and there's something a bit off. She says "Go ahead" even though she's looking at her phone. She briefly lifts her gaze and smiles slightly to encourage him to get on with it. As he makes his case, Joshua can tell that she's just not getting it. It's not that she isn't hearing what he is saying; she isn't listening. After a minute or two, Joshua stops talking. He thinks, "If she's not even going to try to listen, why should I care?"

IMPACT. Joshua feels unheard. He senses he is unappreciated and even betrayed by the person who's supposed to be his boss. Trisha is less than impressed. She's tried to explain to the team that she wants direct, precise, and accurate communication, and Joshua just didn't deliver. Her confidence in Joshua is declining, and Joshua's commitment to Trisha is diminishing. Joshua reported that "I just don't have the energy to give if what I offer isn't valued or wanted. It actually really hurts."

Meeting Scenario 2

This second scenario features Joshua again (whose primary strength is patience) and Trisha again (whose primary strength is dominance).

SITUATION. The situation is the same as above with one exception—the participants have invested the time to consider each other's communication strengths and how they can adapt for a more effective outcome. Joshua prepared an email with an attention-getting subject line and a few bullets explaining the purpose of the meeting. He practiced what he would say— getting to the point that he had a recommendation that would save the company time and money. At the same time, Trisha considered that Josh might benefit from encouragement as opposed to her jumping in to hurry him up. After all, he has been the only one who has taken the time to truly research an option. She takes a few deep breaths, has a pad of paper to take down key points and questions, and decides to give Joshua her full attention.

ACTION. Josh gets right to the point in the session and succinctly describes the solution and anticipated results in a direct, organized manner. Trisha listens attentively, takes a few notes, and nods reassuringly when Joshua pauses. She listens all the way through, and he grows more comfortable sharing the information he had researched. When Joshua has finished, Trisha asks a few follow-up questions and works with him to agree on next steps. She commits to follow up—and she does.

IMPACT. Josh leaves the meeting feeling elated! He believes that his message has been heard and that his hard work has (finally!) paid off. He says, "I think that, for the first time, I'm motivated to contribute more. I didn't realize how amazing it is to feel valued."

Think about a time when you had a positive work experience. It could have been an exceptional conversation, an invitation to be a member of a new team, or a recognition or promotion. If you investigate the root cause of the positive occasion, it probably traces to your being truly listened to and, as a result, your feeling appreciated.

BARRIERS TO PROACTIVE LISTENING

A step toward building CQ for listening is appreciating common barriers or derailers. Think about when that has that happened before. What did you learn? What did you miss? You can minimize such occurrences once you learn to recognize them. Barriers can include:

- **A LACK OF RECOGNITION OF YOUR OWN COMMUNICATION STRENGTHS AND THE COMMUNICATION STRENGTHS OF OTHERS.** As the interactions between Joshua and Trisha illustrate, it is important to understand your strengths and those of others, and adapt as appropriate, to set the stage for effective listening.
- **THE DIFFERENCE BETWEEN SPEED OF THOUGHT AND SPEECH.** There is a conundrum for humans when it comes to listening. It turns out that we are able to process words at a greater speed than the average pace of speaking. According to the National Center for Voice and Speech, the average rate in America for English speakers is about 150 words per minute. Our brains are able to process about 600–800 words per minute. This means that the listener hears faster than the speaker speaks. The gap leads to the brain looking

for something to fill the void. Have you been in a meeting and your mind drifts away from the conversation or presentation to wonder what's for dinner or why Damon chose to wear a tie today? Effective listeners choose to manage the speech-hearing conundrum.

- **INFORMATION OVERLOAD.** This occurs when there is so much being communicated that the listener essentially shuts down, unable to absorb anything more in a meaningful way. This can happen when one-way communication drones on with little or no interaction or interruption. For example, a conference with ten speakers presenting one after the other can be mind-numbing, as can a slew of facts delivered without a break or context.

- **PERSONAL CONCERNS AND DISTRACTIONS.** An employee may have just received good or bad news. Or the employee may be thinking about what to pick up at the store on the way home or a myriad of other thoughts that occupy the human brain. Sounds can also intrude on concentration. A cell phone buzzing, a door slamming, or birds singing outside on a beautiful day are distractions that can limit a focus on being present in the moment to listen.

- **JUDGING AND EVALUATING.** This is a big one. It can occur if someone is entering an interaction with a preconceived outcome. Or a person may make assumptions about the messenger based on the message. Judgments can stem from disagreeing with a message and drawing unfounded conclusions. Having an open and unclouded mind when it comes to evaluating is essential for CQ listening.

Any of these can get in the way, let alone several. It takes time yet is very doable when you know what to look for!

CQ STEPS FOR EFFECTIVE LISTENING

Listening tendencies can vary from person to person. But the good part is that it is a CQ skill and can be developed by following these steps:

- **PREPARE TO LISTEN.** This means taking a deep breath, clearing your mind, and setting your intention. For some meetings, it may mean being prepared to take notes or ensuring someone is assigned this responsibility. It could also involve limiting distractions by following best meeting practices. If as a listener you find yourself being pulled away, you can recognize the distracting thought and refocus on the present. Learn to still the voice within.
- **BE PRESENT AND FOCUSED.** This involves being intentionally and fully conscious of what is going on at the moment. Those who have practiced mindfulness will recognize the full awareness that occurs when you are tuned in objectively and in the present. (And for goodness' sake, turn off the phone.) Maintaining eye contact appropriately is a way to stay present, as well as to let the speaker know you are attentive and taking the message seriously.
- **LISTEN AND THINK FROM ANOTHER'S PERSPECTIVE.** Another's perspective offers insight that you might have missed, thoughts you might not have had, and ideas that could have high value to many others.
- **BE CURIOUS.** Who knows what this meeting, this conversation, or this interaction could reveal to you? You'll never know if you're not open to possibilities. There's something playful and uplifting about having a curious mindset. Bring curiosity to your next conversation, listen well, and see what emerges.
- **LISTEN ALL THE WAY THROUGH (NO INAPPROPRIATE INTERRUPTIONS).** Do you remember the statistics about how we process thoughts faster than people speak? One way that people fill the speaking-hearing gap is that they begin to formulate answers before the question has even been asked. The quality of a response

depends on your listening all the way through to what the speaker is saying and understanding from the speaker's perspective.

- **LISTEN BETWEEN THE LINES.** Listen for the implicit meanings, as well as the explicit ones. Instead of accepting a person's remarks as the entire story, listen for things left unsaid or unexplained. Is there a layer of meaning behind the message? Is this worthy of further investigation? Be attentive not only to what people are saying but also to what they are feeling. This includes interpreting body language to identify what is truly being relayed.

- **CHECK FOR UNDERSTANDING.** We've noted this strategy before as a way to keep yourself engaged and focused. State back in your own words the interpretation of the speaker's message—"So what I hear you saying is . . ." Time this appropriately to break listening into little bites. Good listening involves reciprocity. When someone has really connected with you in a conversation, how do you let the person know? For example, you can say, "I never thought about it like you've just explained. That makes a lot of sense." Checking for understanding along the way in a conversation is a tried-and-true technique that supports proactive listening.

- **BE EMPATHETIC.** As noted in Chapter 9 on empathy, listening involves trying to see a situation through another person's eyes and understanding how that person feels. You can't do this when you're judging the person as he or she is talking. Extend civility, respect, compassion, and grace to the degree that you would like it extended to you. This includes being positive, particularly when initially responding. Resist the temptation to derail an interaction with an evaluative, critical, or disparaging comment at the moment a remark is uttered. When pushback or feedback is helpful, focus on constructive replies about the behavior—not about the person.

ON THE ROAD TO CQ MASTERY—PROACTIVE LISTENING

What can you do to put into practice what you learned in this chapter?

- Consider your communication strengths. Are there ways you can adapt to be a more effective listener?
- Review the list of barriers and improvement tips:
  - What are two areas where you have strong capabilities?
  - What is one development opportunity?
- Choose an upcoming opportunity—a meeting, conversation, or interaction with a particular person—to practice listening skills. What was the experience like?
- Have a conversation with your accountability partner or a colleague, and ask what your partner/colleague thinks about the impact of listening at work. Then listen all the way through to what he or she has to share.

WHAT'S NEXT?

The next chapter focuses on CQ4—expanding safe spaces. Shouldn't each and every one of us know that we can communicate freely and be heard by all in an environment where we know that we belong?

CQ4: EXPANDING
SAFE SPACES

We are talking about spaces where all people
are welcome and valued and know that they belong,
and all well-intentioned communication is heard.
Can all workplaces be safe spaces?

Alice's Adventures in Wonderland is the classic story by Lewis Carroll that was first published in 1865. It's the story of young Alice who goes on an adventure down the rabbit hole and encounters all sorts of diverse and intriguing characters on her journey of self-discovery. *Alice* is the third most quoted piece in the history of literature behind the Bible and the works of William Shakespeare. It has never been out of print since it was published and has been translated into almost 180 different languages. It's also one of the first prominent novels to feature a young woman as the protagonist. During her time in Wonderland, Alice tries to answer the question, "Who am I?" (I don't know about you, but that's a question I'm still asking.) Her search takes her to various locales where she tries to fit in. She adjusts physically (her height varies). She adjusts her communication approach (her questions become more astute). And she offers compassion to all she meets and hopes to have it returned. I like to think that the Cheshire Cat (whom I take to be an introvert) is trying to create a safe space for Alice (whom I view as an extrovert)—a place where she is welcome, has a friend, and is invited to be her true self.

Although there are well-founded policies, research, and theories around the concept of safe spaces which are worth examining, at the heart is an attempt to answer questions we all ask at some point: "Is there a space where I can truly be myself? Where can I express my thoughts and opinions and expect that they will be met with respect? Is there a place where I truly belong?"

WHERE ARE YOU NOW?

In the table below, indicate your level of proficiency in terms of creating safe spaces at work.

LEVEL	BEHAVIORS	WHERE I AM NOW
Novice	I am not familiar with the concept of safe spaces. I want to learn more about my role in the practice.	
Intermediate	I understand why safe spaces can make a difference. I try to communicate to make others feel they belong.	
Mastery	I make it a priority to communicate to ensure all feel that they belong and are welcome and that their emotions and opinions are heard. I know about resources to help others (and myself) if they don't feel safe.	

In this chapter you will:

- Understand the *concept and practice of safe spaces.*
- Consider the *dimensions of diversity* at work.
- Identify *who is responsible* for establishing safe spaces in a work context.
- Explore *steps you can take* to help establish and *maintain a safe space environment for everyone.*

WHAT IS A SAFE SPACE AT WORK?

While there is no firm consensus on the precise origin of the concept of safe spaces, it has been traced to the 1960s and the women's rights movement. It was a way to support and protect a community focused on social reforms and political change.

At work, the term refers to places where all individuals can live their identity free of conflict, criticism, or bias—places where ideas and feelings can be expressed freely without fear of recrimination, backlash, or retaliation.

In one context, these places are designated physical areas that are designed to be safe zones. It's been more challenging to define best practices for safe spaces in the virtual workspace. For some, it's easier to share ideas and feelings when they are in a home environment where they feel comfortable being themselves. Others in the virtual workspace may miss the affirmation of face-to-face interactions and the ability to interpret nonverbal communication, particularly when important or difficult messages are exchanged. In a broader sense, the concept of safe spaces refers to a culture at work, which embodies safe space principles. The purpose of a specific physical room would be voided if the general culture at work—the environment beyond the physical room—didn't fully reflect the rights of all individuals to be safe, valued, and heard.

Even with the best intentions and practices, a safe space culture is not easy in execution. I've heard from many people over the years who have been confused, frustrated, and even frightened by mixed messages from leadership. A line worker in a manufacturing plant shared her experience: "I bought into the idea that I could confide in my manager if I had concerns after the all-employee meeting on safe spaces and the idea that everyone had the right to be themselves. I should have known better than to talk with my manager about how a few of us on the team didn't feel respected and that it was impacting team morale. The response was 'I hear you, but we're behind in our numbers. So suck it up and get to work.'" A necessity is for a culture in theory to be backed up by the words, actions, and attitudes of leaders and managers in practice every day.

Emotions at Work

I recognize that there are a few organizations that imply that their employees should leave their emotions at the door and limit what they do and say to a strict work context. The belief is that this will promote productivity and profits. Give me a break! We are all human. And humans have emotions such as joy, fear, sadness, surprise, and anger. Healthy humans express their emotions in appropriate ways and are supported by their work environments. When individuals are able to express themselves and teams work well together, productivity increases.

It's About Communication

The link between the emotions we feel and our ability to relate them to others, of course, is communication. The fact is that when employees know that they can express themselves and that their voices are heard, they are more engaged.

I recognize that there are detractors of the topic of safe spaces. Some ask that if there are designated safe spaces, does that imply that other spaces aren't safe? Others voice concern that a result may be that employees are coddled in a physical area where their views are unconditionally supported and may not be challenged and discussed, even in a respectful and professional manner. Another view is that safe spaces create a siloed comfort zone—that taking calculated risks and learning from mistakes in a work-related "discomfort" zone is an important way that employees grow professionally. I believe that these views are primarily based on misinformation or misunderstanding of the objectives and principles of safe spaces.

WHAT WE CAN AGREE ON

In working with employees at all levels over decades, I've found that the vast majority agree with the concept of safe spaces. They assert that they wouldn't want to work in an environment where they did not feel welcomed and wouldn't be safely heard. Here are some of the principles on which there is broad consensus:

- All employees have a right to know they belong in, and are welcome in, their work culture and workspace.
- All employees should be valued for who they are and the unique contributions they offer and make.
- All individuals should feel comfortable expressing their emotions to all in a professional, respectful way.
- There should be no question that all employees will be listened to and their messages heard by colleagues, managers, and others in a professional, respectful manner.
- It should the norm that conversations, including challenging ones, can take place at work and opinions can be offered freely without concern of unprofessional judgment or reprisal.
- Safe spaces means that there can be healthy disagreements (not a series of echo chambers that reinforce unilateral opinions).
- In establishing designated safe places, organizations should use best practices in creating attractive, welcoming environments.
- Organizations must have a no-tolerance policy regarding harassment, bullying, and discrimination.

I am encouraged that most agree that an environment where all feel welcome and safe is a necessary goal. A significant benefit of this is that it lends itself to better communications, as well.

DIMENSIONS OF DIVERSITY

Integral to the concept of safe spaces is the recognition that diversity is the cornerstone of any respected enterprise. Embracing diversity, equity, and inclusion (DEI) has always been the right thing to do. However, open conversations around DEI at work have recently emerged with greater frequency and force. Over the decades that I've worked with employees and employers, they've emphasized that DEIB resonates, with the "B" standing for "belonging." A prerequisite for safe spaces is that employees can consider work a place where they can be accepted for who they truly are . . . a space where they *belong* (more on this concept is coming up).

The business case for diversity is supported by a conclusive pool of research. More diverse companies have higher revenues, experience greater innovation, and attract a stronger pool of candidates. Their employees perform better, and they can reach new and more diverse markets.

In considering the aspects of diversity, it is valuable to recognize the depth and breadth of DEI dimensions. In essence, we are talking about the aspects of individual identities, which can have common elements and unique combinations. Here are several dimensions to consider related to diversity. Which ones do you relate to?

- **COMMUNICATION INTELLIGENCE.** A core dimension is our differing CQ strengths and combinations of strengths. As emphasized earlier, these involve natural tendencies and preferences that shape other dimensions, and are shaped by them, over time.
- **PROTECTED DIMENSIONS.** Under federal law in the United States, employers cannot discriminate on the basis of race, national origin, sex, age, disability, or religion.
- **CHOSEN DIMENSIONS.** Most individuals have options that they may choose to exercise at different times in their lives. These include educational level, marital status, places to live, talents to develop as part of our identity (e.g., sports, arts). What are other items you would include in this category?
- **PROFESSIONALLY RELATED DIMENSIONS.** The number of options when it comes to our professional identities is expanding. These include your occupational sector, the level and title of your job, and your choice of belonging, or not, to a union. It also includes your workspace—whether you work virtually, in a hybrid environment, or in an in-person workspace. It can involve your employment status—whether you are a full-time employee, self-employed, a gig employee, or retired.

CQ TAKEAWAYS. In DEI initiatives, which may include establishing a safe space culture, a primary focus is often on the protected dimensions that include race, gender, and sexual orientation. It's important to recognize that how we are treated and valued at work frequently ties to other organizational dimensions. As with our heroine in *Alice's Adventures in Wonderland*, the answer to "Who am I?" may be complex and involve multiple aspects, many of which can vary over time.

WHO'S RESPONSIBLE FOR SAFE SPACES?

There are several correct answers to this important question:

- In a legal sense, employers and organizations are responsible for maintaining a nonhostile environment where harassment, bullying, and discrimination are not tolerated. They are held accountable when there *is* a hostile environment where these behaviors are allowed. This is defined in law and enforced by the federal Equal Employment Opportunity Commission (EEOC). Most organizations have written policies and procedures to follow when employees perceive they are harassed, bullied, or discriminated against.
- At the organizational level, leaders are largely responsible for establishing a safe space culture and environment. They have the opportunity to let it be known that all individuals are welcome, are valued, belong, and will be heard. Leaders should set the example by their words and actions.
- At the foundational level, each and every individual is responsible for supporting a safe space environment at work. You have the opportunity to make a major impact on the well-being of others through your actions every day. For example, the choice of where and how to have conversations is increasingly the choice of employees.

WHAT CAN I DO TO PROMOTE A SAFE SPACE ENVIRONMENT?

Respect and rapport play a significant role in creating the space others find most comfortable.

Make Others Feel Like They Belong

As noted earlier, employees need to know that they matter, and that their needs matter, not only the needs of the company. How can you help others connect purpose to their professional lives? We should act on the premise that humans crave purpose and meaningful work. The result, of course, is higher morale and productivity. Each and every individual wants to belong.

Other CQ essentials are tied to making others feel like they belong. The two previous chapters on balancing empathy and proactive listening describe powerful strategies for expanding safe spaces.

Hone Your Situational Awareness

Like many aspects of CQ, being part of solutions thinking regarding safe spaces starts with awareness. If you haven't had the concept of safe spaces on your radar screen, turn up your detector by exploring these questions:

- When you observe the verbal and non-verbal communication of colleagues, do you believe they feel fully comfortable and encouraged to express their opinions? Do you feel fully comfortable expressing your opinions?
- In meetings, for example, are others listened to and fully heard in a professional sense? Are you?
- Are there those who feel "less than" in terms of respect for their work contributions?

With this awareness, you can be an ally and listen in to those who may feel left out. One way to do this is to acknowledge diversity in communication strengths. Embrace the individuality of your colleagues. An environment of expansive safe spaces is measured by genuine and consistent rapport, respect, curiosity, and interpersonal productivity that builds trust.

Have Regular Communication

Lack of communication can lead to confusion and emotions such as suspicion and fear. You can choose to proactively communicate even when others choose to be silent.

Resolve Open Issues Promptly

Communication can be particularly important when there are unresolved issues on the table. What may be insignificant to some may be perceived as paramount to others. When you identify open issues and communicate with the intent to promote understanding, it helps build an environment of openness where others feel freer to express themselves.

Be Aware of Resources to Help

Mental health support at work is an imperative, which can involve providing resources to help with prevention and treatment. When you are aware of what is available and how to access options, you are better prepared to help yourself and others. Here are some resources you can call on:

- **EMPLOYEE ASSISTANCE PROGRAMS (EAPS).** Does your organization have an employee assistance program? According to the US Department of Labor's Bureau of Labor Statistics, the majority of employers do, and the programs are more prevalent among larger organizations. The purpose of an EAP is to help employees (and frequently their families) who are in a crisis or other stressful situation.
- **ANTI-HARASSMENT, ANTI-BULLYING, AND ANTI-DISCRIMINATION POLICIES AND PROCEDURES.** As stated above, harassment, bullying, and discrimination are not to be tolerated in the workspace. Most employers should have related policies and

procedures. For more information, visit the US Department of Labor's EEOC (at eeoc.gov).

Create Your Own Safe Space and Wellness Habits

What are practices that you can undertake on a regular basis to help promote your wellness? A growing number of employers offer options ranging from exercise to stress reduction programs and meditation/mindfulness options. You may want to have a friend or ally that you check in with on a regular basis. There are free resources on the internet. Do you enjoy and feel less stressed by listening to music, doing art, playing sports, or learning something new? These practices can be included in wellness regimens. Making it a habit to take a few deep breaths or a short walk can help promote a sense of safety and well-being at work.

ON THE ROAD TO CQ MASTERY—
EXPANDING SAFE SPACES

If safe spaces have not been on your radar screen, now is the time to turn up your detector and become situationally aware:

- Do others feel like they belong at work? Do you?
- What is your organization's commitment to a safe space culture—is it at a novice, intermediate, or mastery level?
- What steps can you take to promote a safe workspace?
- Are you aware of resources available to help yourself (and others)?

WHAT'S NEXT?

The next chapter is on CQ5—communicating with challenging people. Is it the person or the behavior that you perceive as challenging? There is almost always common ground if you're open to finding it.

CQ5: COMMUNICATING WITH CHALLENGING PEOPLE

Is it the person or the behavior
that you perceive as challenging?

Communicating with challenging people is one of the most critical aspects of Communication Intelligence. The perception of difficult people has always been a major complication in the workspace, and unless handled well, it drains significant time, energy, and expertise. It is one of the most popular areas that people want help with.

Consider these two pieces of intelligence related to people and work:

- According to the Society for Human Resource Management (SHRM), the number one thing that makes us happy at work is positive relationships—above salary, perks, or flexibility.
- The vast majority of employees report that we deal with difficult people at work.

This means that the vast majority of workers are trying to deal with the very challenge that threatens to derail their source of positive engagement at work. That said, interacting with people that you perceive as challenging is part of work and life. It is inevitable. If challenges are constructively resolved, there are multiple positive benefits including a healthier work environment, happier relationships, and the innovation and progress that can come from constructive conflict resolution.

WHERE ARE YOU NOW?

Where are you now in terms of your proficiency level of communicating with challenging people? Take the self-assessment survey below to find out.

LEVEL	DESCRIPTORS	WHERE I AM NOW
Novice	I avoid confrontation and challenging people as much as I can.	
Intermediate	I try to find common ground with challenging people and communicate with an intent to understand.	
Mastery	I recognize that it usually is a person's behaviors that I find challenging. I have tools—including an understanding of different communication strengths—to interact well with challenging people in almost all circumstances.	

In this chapter you will:

- Distinguish between *challenging people* and *challenging behaviors*.
- Recognize that communicating with those you perceive as challenging *begins with self-awareness*.
- Apply specific strategies such as *communication strengths, the five-why model, and clarifying conversations*.

CHALLENGING PEOPLE OR CHALLENGING BEHAVIORS?

Is there someone that you struggle with and feel uncomfortable being near? A first step is to recognize that there is something that underlies the discomfort. That *something* may be related to differences in communication strengths and not the actual person. After all, does the person that is your nemesis have friends, other people to hang out with, or family members who seem to tolerate the person or even enjoy the person's company? Let's face it; there most likely has been a time when you were the person that someone else described as difficult. Maybe you weren't even aware of the dynamic that your behavior had set in motion.

In thinking of that colleague who is troublesome, consider if the situation is due to a one-off exchange or an ongoing tense relationship. If the person was having a bad day and reacted in the stress of the moment, it's probably best to shake it off.

However, if you believe that what you are experiencing is persisting and, in fact, growing worse over time, impacting the productivity of you and/or the team, and you currently see no obvious solution, then it's time to analyze the circumstances, consider your options, and take action. If you are someone who struggles with taking action, that is OK. In some cases it is helpful to involve a third party to advocate on your behalf because it is unlikely that the situation will resolve itself.

WHAT IS CHALLENGING YOU?

Each communication strength brings opportunities and challenges related to interacting with those who have different strengths from yours. If you've decided that it's time to take action to resolve the situation, it's time to gain clarity. Below is a five-step process to support you toward this goal:

1. **DO A SELF-ANALYSIS.** Are your communication strengths contributing to the situation?
2. **ASSESS THE PERSON'S BEHAVIOR.** What are the person's communication strengths, and how do you interact?
3. **DO A ROOT CAUSE ANALYSIS: THE FIVE WHYS.** This is a process that leads you toward understanding why you perceive the situation and/or behavior as challenging.

4. **ASK FOR AN OUTSIDE OPINION.** This will help validate your analysis from a third-party perspective.

5. **DRAW AN ASSESSMENT CONCLUSION.** This should be the best attempt to define the challenge at this stage with the information you have.

After working through the steps, you should have more objective clarity and be better positioned to make some decisions toward resolution. Let's take a closer look at these suggestions:

1. Do a Self-Analysis

The place to begin on the road to resolution is to look in the mirror. Before beginning a self-analysis, start the process by naming the person and situation. Who is the person with the challenging behavior, and what is your professional relationship (e.g., colleague, boss, customer?). For most, this will be a current situation. For some, this may be a challenging relationship from years or even decades past that still brings up strong and unresolved emotions. Identify the person and situation in writing:

Name/relationship: _____

What is the challenging behavior that comes to mind?

_____

_____

_____

Consider your CQ strengths and how you are adapting in the current environment. What is the impact on you of the situation with this person? What is the impact on your behavior? Are there related emotions? For example:

- Are you ignoring the person or avoiding conversations or situations?
- Are you worried? Stressed? Frustrated? Angry? Unhappy?

- Does the situation make you question yourself? Feel something is wrong with you?
- Are you not as effective at work as you'd like to be?

It's important for all of us to remember that relationships involve at least two people—and in this case, you are one of them. It's time to take responsibility, if appropriate. What are *you doing* to contribute to the challenging aspects of the relationship?

2. Assess the Person's Communication Strengths

Now consider the person's communication strengths and how he or she may be adapting. Put yourself in the person's shoes.

Before labeling an individual as "difficult," take time to consider that perhaps what you are experiencing is simply a "communication strengths clash." Recognizing and understanding the potential for challenges between the strengths and letting that influence your communication choices is an important aspect of CQ. Below are potential pitfalls that can occur between strengths:

- **DOMINANT AND NON-DOMINANT (HOW YOU GET RESULTS).** A potential pitfall between these two strengths is the dominant individual's requirement for direct and concise communication in looking for the problem to solve. The non-dominant individual prefers giving the full context of a situation and is often only looking for input and collaboration toward the bottom-line result.
- **EXTROVERT AND INTROVERT (YOUR PEOPLE PREFERENCE).** A potential pitfall between these two strengths is that the extrovert individual thrives on relational harmony and the introvert individual can sometimes be difficult to read or is even restrained in some interactions, especially in a group setting. It can feel like pulling teeth to get an introvert individual to take part in brainstorming, for example, because he or she does not like to be put on the spot and may feel uncomfortable or pressured.

- **AMBIVERT AND BOTH EXTROVERT/INTROVERT (YOUR PEOPLE PREFERENCE).** A potential pitfall between these strengths is the mislabeling of the ambivert as being moody. Because the ambivert moves easily between extroversion and introversion, it can be challenging to understand what the ambivert is thinking or feeling without that person's ability to communicate as such.
- **PATIENT AND IMPATIENT (HOW YOU PACE YOURSELF).** A potential pitfall between these two strengths is that the impatient individual can view the patient individual as being lazy and can get frustrated when things are not completed in what the impatient person considers to be an appropriate timeline. As well, the patient individual likes time to think before answering, so if pressured into an immediate response, the patient person will most likely default just to appease the impatient person for the moment.
- **CONFORMIST AND NON-CONFORMIST (YOUR ATTENTION TO DETAILS/SYSTEMS).** A potential pitfall between these two strengths lies in the approach. A non-conformist individual does not like to be micromanaged and prefers to find his or her own way to results. This can be frustrating to a conformist individual, who believes that there is a distinct right and wrong way of doing things and prefers step-by-step detailed processes.

AN IMPORTANT NOTE ON HARASSMENT, DISCRIMINATION, AND BULLYING. To reemphasize, if you believe the behavior that you identified would be considered harassment, discrimination, or bullying, this is an extremely serious matter that you should not work through by yourself. We also need to remember there's a difference between clashing communication and harassment, discrimination, or bullying. That said, these unacceptable behaviors can happen, and yet you or others might not immediately recognize it as such until someone else points it out. The organization that you are working for, or working with, should have policies in place to address this unacceptable behavior. Please follow the process and communicate the circumstance to your boss or a human resources representative for the appropriate actions to resolve the problem and to ensure you are safe in the workspace. Another resource for information is the EEOC of the US Department of Labor: https://www.eeoc.gov/harassment.

3. Do a Root Cause Analysis—the Five Whys

Many times, at work and in life, we are asked to problem-solve. Most employers cite problem solving as a desirable competency associated with high performers. An often-overlooked prerequisite, however, is problem finding. (As noted earlier, there is a path here to solutions thinking.)

For this analysis, take a deep breath and try to have an open mind. The technique is called the five whys, and if you haven't heard of it, know that it's a proven method used in manufacturing and other sectors to find solutions and explore the causes underlying a particular challenge—to identify the root cause. It was developed by Sakichi Toyoda, the founder of Toyota Industries, in the 1930s and is a featured component of Lean Manufacturing, Kaizen, and Six Sigma. For our purposes, we will adapt the technique to apply to the situation you've identified.

There are no specific rules about where the series of questions—the five whys—will lead or whether you will end up with one specific root cause. As is the case with any aspect of self-reporting, it will depend in large part on what emerges in your answers. In any case, the process should be helpful in clarifying the communication challenge you are experiencing with your colleague.

A few guidelines:

- **MAKE SURE THE QUESTION IS FRAMED ABOUT YOU**—after all, you can only honestly reflect from your experience—not someone else's. For example, "Why am I so unnerved by Bob's behavior?" versus "Why does Bob always try to annoy me?" Try to focus on knowledge and facts (versus feelings and emotions).
- **IDENTIFY BEHAVIORS VERSUS THE PERSON.** For example, let's say that normally reliable Jean doesn't respond to an email request in a timely manner. You *could* frame the issue as "This is unusual for Jean. Something may be going on that I'm not aware of"—focusing on her behavior—instead of "Jean is totally undependable. I can't

trust her with anything." The latter likely unfairly summarizes the character of Jean in a personal manner with broad, unconstructive implications. Focusing on the specific behavior is more likely to lead to a manageable resolution and keeps it in the professional realm.

Approach this with a positive and sincere mindset. The case has been made about the importance of mindset earlier. Being as objective as possible, without a predetermined conclusion, and with an intention of achieving a positive outcome is much more likely to set you up for a successful resolution than having a negative, biased outlook from the start.

The process involves asking a series of five whys. The answer to each question will provide a basis for the next, each one leading closer to a root cause.

Here's an example:

SITUATION. Julie, my boss, is getting on my nerves. She keeps saying that we'll sit down and talk about a raise, and it never happens.

PROBLEM. Julie keeps ignoring me when it comes to talking about a raise. It really bugs me.

1. Why? Because this is an important issue for me, and she knows it.
2. Why? I need to get a sense of what I should expect from her.
3. Why? I need her support if I'm going to stay and succeed in my job and on our team.
4. Why? I need to have the right expectations going forward.
5. Why? With clear expectations, I can adapt if I need to improve and become better at my job.

Now, it's your turn. Ask yourself five whys, and write your answers in your CQ journal or in another convenient place. If, at this point, you have some clarity about potential action you can take, a next step in the five whys process is to answer a next question—how?—as in "How can I constructively take action to improve the situation?"

EXAMPLE. How? This has to do more with me than Julie. I will handle this professionally. I will get on her calendar through the app (versus asking her). I will have specific questions in order to understand her expectations. Then I can make a personal plan to alter my behavior and succeed.

4. Ask for an Outside Opinion

If you choose to act on this step, it can provide additional perspective and help advance your thinking toward a solution. Select a person whom you respect, who is not too close to the situation, and whom you believe will handle your situation with confidentiality. This could be your accountability partner or another colleague or friend.

5. Draw an Assessment Conclusion

With the steps you have taken so far, are you feeling more in control of the situation than before this assessment exercise? If so, that's an indication that you are on a good path toward constructively addressing the challenging behavior. At this point, it is likely that your analysis falls into one of three categories:

- **COMMUNICATION CHALLENGE AND OPPORTUNITY.** Particularly in the workplace, conflicting communication strengths are a culprit of strained relationships. Unless you both are extremely self-aware and motivated to understand the other's strengths and their implications, tension and conflict are probably going to emerge. This also can occur when two people have different beliefs or value anchors.
- **SITUATIONAL CHALLENGES.** There are workspace stressors and pressures—lack of clear goals, managers who are not self-aware, unreasonable time pressure, or other engagement derailers—that fuel conflict. These also are potential areas of common ground.
- **ANNOYING BEHAVIOR.** Is the culprit annoying or obnoxious behavior? Maybe (now that you think about it), it's not that big a deal. With a little effort, can you acknowledge it and adapt your attitude or behavior without the person's behavior provoking you negatively?

Next-Step Options

With an analysis and more objective description of the challenge, a next step is to identify an option that you believe will lead toward a resolution. As alluded to earlier, you can't change someone else, so an "I wish he would just behave and think differently" won't work. Take it out of the personal groove and understand that there is greater good at the end of the journey.

However, if you are conflicted or hesitant or fearful of what might happen next, think of the longer-term positives—working through these hard steps will lead to more energy, clarity, and liberation. Your investment also could result in better self-understanding, a stronger relationship, or at least a better grasp of the situation.

SIX ADDITIONAL STRATEGIES

Which of the following six strategies make sense for you at this time? Are other options popping up?

1. Use Clarifying Conversations

The purpose of a clarifying conversation (an effective strategy in most circumstances) is to, as objectively as possible, address the issues that are causing tension and, if possible, identify steps that can be taken to ease or progress the situation. You can only act with good faith on your end—the other person may not even know there is an issue.

The strategy is to stay away from assumption and subjectivity, positively (not defensively) address facts, and see if there can be a meeting of the minds. An objective is to, at the end of the session, have clarity on both sides of potential next steps and leave no confusion, hard feelings, or unanswered questions or issues. This requires both parties accepting personal responsibility, and as the initiator, you can only do so much. Here are a few steps:

- **SET THE REASON FOR THE MEETING.** Be as clear as possible on the objective for the clarifying conversation, and frame it in a work context. (Please note that "venting" is not a good objective.) For example, "I want to reach an understanding with Carmen about how I can help ensure the next meeting is productive."

- **INVITE THE PERSON TO MEET.** Given what you know about the other person's communication strengths, would an email (possible subject line: "Good Time to Talk?"), text, phone message, or in-person invite work best to set the stage for a productive session? Set a time limit on the meeting to help ensure the conversation has a beginning, middle, and end.
- **INVITE A THIRD PERSON.** An option in some cases is to have a third person present. This may be important if you anticipate the session could benefit from an objective listener. Please make sure you and the other person are on the same page regarding inviting the additional participant.

It's time for the meeting. Here are a few best practice tips:

- **START WITH, AND LOOK FOR, COMMON GROUND.** What are the larger goals that you both have in common? For example, that might be: "I know we both like working here and want our team to succeed. What do you think?" (The other person agrees.) Then follow up: "A key to our success will be that we take time to communicate clearly to help everyone be on the same page. What do you think?"
- **LISTEN PROACTIVELY.** Proactive listening is another CQ essential. Ask open-ended, positively intended questions, and listen all the way through.
- **FILTER AND REFOCUS.** Depending on how the conversation goes, you may have to call on your self-awareness and filter out comments that could trigger uncomfortable emotions. If the other person responds with what you perceive as a personal attack, refocus your mindset and the conversation on the common goal.

As the end of the meeting time approaches, *steer the conversation to a positive conclusion.* Even if you don't see eye to eye on everything, are you able to reach agreement on one or two action steps? For example, "At the next meeting, we will be on the same page regarding our common interest in ensuring we have adequate resources."

Set a time for a follow-up conversation to build more common ground over positive momentum, and set the stage for further resolution.

If a clarifying conversation is not an option or did not produce positive results, here are few more strategies.

2. Adapt Your Behavior

If there is no interest or awareness on the other person's part, all you can do is adjust your behavior and attitude. What can you do? Are there boundaries you can set? For example, proactively go about your work, and define when and how you will interact with this person. This may involve not engaging in chitchat before a meeting and keeping conversations to strictly professional topics.

CQ TIP. You can also apply the ADAPT model from Chapter 3.

3. Agree to Disagree

In a world where there may be strong differences in values, political views, and issues that unavoidably spill over into the workspace, you may have to acknowledge areas of differences and be fine with that. The key is that you are now aware of the issue and in control of how you choose to respond.

4. Ignore the Person

There may be cases when the other person is intent on pushing your buttons and is fueled by the fact that you react. Ignore the person's behavior, be nonreactive, and see if the lack of fuel diminishes or eliminates the behavior.

5. Know When to Walk Away

Your instinct may be to try to "fix" the situation or the person by investing an uncomfortable amount of time and energy. As has been noted, you can't change other people, so don't knock your head against the wall. The best option may be to stop trying to fix things, walk away, and invest your valuable energy in something far more productive.

6. Find Appropriate Support

This may involve escalating an issue to a boss or lead; be sure to frame the issue in a business context after you have done your homework.

ON THE ROAD TO CQ MASTERY— COMMUNICATING WITH CHALLENGING PEOPLE

There are a lot of options to consider in this chapter. Try different strategies in different situations to see what works. Have a conversation with your accountability partner about his or her experiences. What can you learn and apply together?

WHAT'S NEXT?

The next CQ chapter is on giving and receiving feedback, which is essential for the development and success of individuals, relationships, and organizations. Why is it so difficult for so many?

CHAPTER
13

CQ6: RECEIVING AND
GIVING ONGOING FEEDBACK

The vast majority of workers want,
welcome, and even crave feedback.
Why is it so difficult for most to receive and give?

Feedback, delivered constructively and with strengths in mind, is designed to improve future actions and performance. From the day we're born until we die, we need feedback to learn, evolve, survive, and (with persistence) flourish. And it's everywhere, if we are open to seeing and receiving it! For example, a child may get feedback from touching a hot stove—it hurts! It's best to avoid that behavior. In school, students receive feedback in terms of grades, reviews, and evaluations that guide their learning. At work, giving and receiving feedback is essential for the development and success of individuals, relationships, and organizations. However, study after study finds that traditional communication, which focuses on identifying how someone is *not* performing—pointing out weaknesses and "areas for improvement"—is counterproductive.

So, what can be done about it? In my experience, getting feedback in the moment—or close to it—is received as helpful rather than getting it once a year when the person on the receiving end is seriously questioning why this was not shared much earlier. The next best practice is getting feedback quarterly, and lastly having an informal review six months prior to the formal review so there is time for the receiver to act on it. All this said, the sincerity of the feedback is critical. The provider is best served adapting to the style of the receiver as much as possible. And best to start out with what is working, then moving into specific areas that need improvement.

WHERE ARE YOU NOW?

What is your current level of proficiency in terms of giving and receiving feedback?

LEVEL	DESCRIPTORS	WHERE I AM NOW
Novice	I'm not comfortable receiving or giving feedback.	
Intermediate	I follow the rules and policies when it comes to feedback.	
Mastery	I look forward to, and act on, feedback I receive. I ask for feedback when appropriate. I offer constructive feedback to others when I believe it would be useful.	

In this chapter, you will:

- Validate why most of us are *not comfortable* with receiving and giving traditional feedback.
- Discover why most *want and even crave feedback.*
- Define *different types* of feedback and a *feedback loop.*
- Identify your *primary feedback provider.* (*Hint:* Look in the mirror!)
- Prioritize *best practices* for feedback—as a receiver, as a giver, and in terms of teams and organizations.

WHAT'S THE BIG DEAL ABOUT FEEDBACK?

If there ever was a not "once and done" in the CQ space, this is it.

Most of Us Have a Problem *Giving* Feedback in a Work Context

Employees who have "giving feedback" in their job descriptions tend to believe it's among the most challenging aspects of their job, because while they are expected to do it, few are trained in how to do it. Many say they would rather fire someone, because at least you can get on the other side quickly and move on, rather than accepting that "giving feedback" is a skill set they need to acquire sooner than later. At Forté we begin that process with the Forté Interaction Report given to the reviewer and receiver in advance of the review. Specifics are provided on how both best adapt to the other to get the message across most productivity. The Forté Interaction Report is our most popular report, for all the right reasons.

For the employees tasked with giving feedback, the rationales for not wanting to engage in performance conversations include the following:

- **THERE MAY BE A NEGATIVE REACTION.** For example, they might think: "They won't like me" or "What if they cry or get angry?" or "What if they tell other people I was mean to them?"
- **THEY DON'T SEE THAT IT'S NECESSARY.** For example, they might think: "Jason is a professional. He should know what to do."
- **IT'S NOT IN THEIR COMFORT ZONE, AND THEY AVOID IT AT ALL COST.** For example, they might think: "I'm not good at that touchy-feely part of my job."
- **THEY'VE NEVER BEEN TOLD WHY IT'S IMPORTANT OR TRAINED HOW TO OFFER IT.** As a result, they might think it is not that important, and so the lack of preparation and delivery does more damage than good.
- **THERE'S A CULTURAL BIAS AGAINST FEEDBACK.** In other words, some cultures are more inclined toward direct feedback than others. For example, they might think: "This is a waste of time. What do 'they' know?!" And little intake from the feedback session is even heard, let alone acted upon.

Work-related feedback, of course, isn't just a function between leaders and employees. There is peer-to-peer feedback, informal feedback, and feeding up to a supervisor. (More on this later.)

Employees Have a Problem *Receiving* Feedback

It seems that many employees are uncomfortable with, and even fear, feedback.

The fear factor is associated with negativity. If people hear anything except praise and top performance ratings, they may feel like they are being criticized and are valued less than counterparts. When they hear how they didn't live up to someone else's expectations and their perceived weaknesses are pointed out and written down, it can lead to feelings of shame and self-doubt (which many will avoid at all cost). When you add in threatened promotions and salaries, reviews can lead to declines in engagement and performance.

One explanation is that as kids, some were taught that they need to get top grades or be the best at a sport or other activity. The "Everyone gets a trophy" mantra doesn't meld well with the realities of the professional world. And the perceived threat of "losing" through being compared to others instead of being valued for one's unique strengths can undermine constructive intent.

Another reason feedback can be a stress factor is that, for decades, many companies used feedback to force employees into unnatural behavior. The "old-school" treatment of workers as cogs in a wheel as opposed to company assets characterized sectors such as industrial manufacturing. The "We're going to improve your weakness" instead of "We're going to build on your strengths" mentality dominated. The annual review was misused by bosses to punish some employees and favor others. There are companies that used reviews as a rationale to rank and weed out "poorer performers."

The fact is that feedback programs and processes as traditionally applied rarely achieve the objective of more engaged, productive employees and improved retention. So, no wonder there is trepidation about receiving and giving feedback. But at the same time, we naturally want it!

Employees Value Feedback as the Key to Professional and Personal Growth

Research shows that the vast majority of workers want, welcome, and even crave feedback at work. According to Gallup's "State of the Global Workplace: 2022 Report," 68 percent of those surveyed say they would commit to working harder if their efforts were better acknowledged. The number is higher for millennials; Gallup also reports that almost 90 percent of this generation indicate that "professional or career growth and development opportunities" are important to them. (Only 15 percent strongly agree, however, that they *ask* for feedback on a regular basis.) A safe conclusion is that employees desire feedback, but not in the way it is generally communicated.

CLOSING THE GIVER-RECEIVER GAP

Harvard researchers found that a key to closing the gap between those who want feedback and those who deliver it is understanding the positive value of feedback. The challenge may be that we don't understand how vital it is. The Harvard study concludes that "the more consequential the feedback, the more likely those in a position to offer feedback were to underestimate how much the recipient desired feedback and the less likely they were to offer it." This is important to understand; never underestimate the recipient's want and need to know the pathway to improvement.

The researchers also found that a little empathy goes a long way. Asking, "If you were in this person's shoes, would you want feedback?" helps provide motivation. In other words, if the feedback providers assume that there is no value to feedback, they can justify postponing or ignoring this responsibility. However, it they count themselves among the vast majority who are looking for effective feedback and consider the higher purpose of improvement over their personal discomfort, this may help close the giver-receiver gap.

Types of Feedback at Work

There are primarily two types of performance feedback—formal and informal.

- **FORMAL FEEDBACK.** Formal processes include annual or periodic reviews where managers provide structured feedback that usually tracks performance against goals and targets. The more formal strategies can include recognition programs or disciplinary processes. These generally are guided by organizational policies and have related documentation. They can involve assessments such as behavioral, technical skill, or 360-rater instruments. (A Gallup study found that 14 percent of employees said that annual reviews motivate them to improve how they approach work. There's probably room to look for a better way.)
- **INFORMAL FEEDBACK.** Informal feedback comes about through everyday conversation and communication. Managers may engage in timely on-the job coaching, peers may provide feedback on what they are observing about a colleague's performance, and team meetings may include opportunities to offer recognition or suggestions for improvement. Research shows that there can be more value in informal than formal communication in that it tends to be more timely, specific, relevant, and actionable. This typically is a best time, as the message is better heard in this environment. The feedback is seen as genuinely and sincerely given and not "judgmental."

The Feedback Loop

The feedback loop is a process where employees give and receive feedback on an ongoing basis. Everyone is involved—up, down, and across an organization. This is what a loop might look like:

- Employees receive timely feedback from managers and colleagues.
- Employees are invited to offer feedback to leaders and peers.
- Leaders establish a culture of sustained communication related to performance and actively participate in the process.

- The general tone is to encourage positive feedback, building on strengths and tied to maximizing individual potential as well as positive organizational outcomes.

Employee feedback loops can be empowering to employees, are beneficial to short- and long-term organizational goals, and build on the best of the formal and informal processes.

BEST PRACTICES FOR FEEDBACK

Below are some best practices for receiving feedback and giving feedback and some recommendations for leaders and organizations to consider. There is overlap among the items. For example, a receiving tip may have relevance for givers, a giver tip may be of interest to receivers and leaders, and so on. You may want to review all the information, regardless of your current position, to help advance your CQ and position yourself for feedback mastery.

For Feedback Receivers

YOU ARE YOUR PRIMARY FEEDBACK PROVIDER. You wake up in the morning and check your messages. What is the first one that you receive? Maybe it's that the day ahead is an open page, waiting for you to write the story: "Today is an opportunity to control what I can, to adapt to whatever situation comes my way, and to give and to grow with others." Or is the message that you messed up yesterday: "It's bound to be another stressful day with matters spinning out of my control. I'd rather just crawl back under the covers and hibernate until the weekend."

You've gotten the point by now. Your primary feedback provider is you. The key is that you, for the most part, have control over what those messages are. It may take some effort to focus on the positive, but there it is! What will you choose? Make it a point to intentionally provide positive feedback to yourself, and the results may amaze you. This is *very* important to understand and do. Yes, we all have areas of improvement and have made mistakes along

COMMUNICATION INTELLIGENCE

the way. Taking a step further, always keep in mind what you learned from the mistake or feedback and definitely reinforce what you are doing well.

HAVE AN OPEN MINDSET—TAKE IT PROFESSIONALLY, NOT PERSONALLY. The teeter-totter of feedback involves recognizing that we may not always hear what we *want* to hear. However, what is being offered may be what we *need* to hear to reach our professional objectives. When the messaging offered is realistic, performance-based, and fair, then take it seriously but not personally.

For those who tend to be less thick-skinned, this may take more of an effort. The first instinct may be to jump into a defensive mode or one of denial. You can adapt through the mental discipline of filtering out any negative perceptions to realize the gold nuggets. For example, a colleague asks for a moment of your time and then says, "You know how much I value you as a team member, and we've worked together for more than a year now. I have to be honest—you just weren't prepared at the meeting yesterday, and it showed. I felt let down, and frankly, we were counting on you to close the deal."

Instead of explaining that your kid was up all night, that you slept through the alarm clock, and that your toothbrush broke, take a deep breath and assume your best professional stance. You could say, "I know; it was just one of those days. I hope you know that it's not my norm. I can't repair the past, but I will commit to do better in the future. May we work together on the next presentation to be sure it meets all our expectations?" This approach explains that you learned from the experience, are taking responsibility for your actions, and are preparing to improve behavior. Accepting and explaining the truth always trumps an "excuse" or playing the blame game.

ASK FOR FEEDBACK! The majority of people do not believe they receive useful feedback communication and don't ask for it. So become comfortable with asking!

There can be a bit of a balancing act here, because we're talking about initiating useful, timely, focused, and efficient conversation to help you improve your performance. We are *not* talking about asking vague, too-frequent questions just to receive external affirmation and to feed a needy ego. For example, your manager drops by and says, "That was a good job at the meeting yesterday." That's fine. However, she didn't provide actionable information you can use, did she? You can follow up by saying, "Thank you! Could you be specific about what you observed that worked? It would help me improve in the future." The keys are to:

- Be positive and receptive by thanking her.
- Ask an open-ended question versus inviting a yes-no response.
- Explain why—that her answer will help you and the team (in other words, it will help make her job easier).
- And then thank her again and be as specific as possible about how you will apply the information.

These steps will be highly beneficial to you and demonstrate your seeking the deeper knowledge and value of the learning opportunity.

Ask colleagues, team members, and/or your accountability partner for feedback. Most people will be glad to help as long as you choose an appropriate time (e.g., not when they are crashing on a deadline) and you reciprocate. As one who recognizes the value of receiving feedback, you should welcome the opportunity to offer feedback.

For Feedback Providers

CATCH THEM DOING SOMETHING RIGHT. Focusing the majority of feedback on what's wrong, when someone makes a mistake, or on all that is negative is so old-school. Think about a time when you received a big old talking-to about what you should be doing that you aren't. Mostly negative. I'll bet you left the conversation feeling pretty discouraged and less than motivated. Now, think about receiving positive feedback about something you did or accomplished. It probably was a motivator.

Ensure the positive feedback is timely and specific. Also, consider applying this strategy with peers and leaders. Who doesn't want positive feedback when it is useful and deserved?

You might want to practice the "catch them doing something right" process with your immediate team to get a feel for it. It is a learned skill that can be extremely beneficial to your work and personal life.

A LESSON FROM LANDRY

Tom Landry was the legendary head football coach of the Dallas Cowboys who served for 29 seasons and won 20 of them along with two Super Bowl rings. Landry's legend expands to the way he provided performance feedback to his team. He observed that players weren't necessarily motivated to perform better just based on a diet of praise and "atta boys." Instead, Landry believed that individuals would be more likely to improve if they knew their personal strengths and how those strengths translated to accomplishment.

So, here's what he did: Instead of the traditional practice of having the team review game films, he compiled individual reels for each player composed of their most successful plays on the field. This way, each team member could view in slow motion what his personal version of excellence looked like and how it contributed to winning.

Would you be motivated by similar personalized, specific feedback tied to your excellence?

The point here is to make it a practice to watch for when someone is doing something right—it could be a seemingly small action that made a difference. Communicate in a timely fashion what the action was, what the positive difference it made was, and why you and/or the team value this contribution. You will emphasize a competency that is already there that can be re-created and continuously improved. And the recipient will likely tell others. You are not judging or trying to change him or her. You are speaking the truth with purpose, and that can be extremely empowering. This is not an overnight learning; it does take practice as mentioned earlier. Yet once this becomes a common and natural skill, you may well become the go-to person on the team.

PROVIDE ONGOING FEEDBACK. We mentioned that decentralized feedback, building on the best of formal and informal practices, can accelerate the positive impact you can offer as a provider.

This can be a simple process that doesn't take as much time as you think, and it can yield strong benefits in terms of team performance and outcomes. To make it work:

- First, recognize the value of ongoing feedback (instead of just a scheduled review).
- Then, try it out! If you're uncertain or uncomfortable, conduct your own pilot study. Identify a period of time (a few days) in which to provide ongoing feedback to a few employees, and observe the behavior change. You may have to adapt your approach to be more effective and confident. It will be worth the investment.

MEET OTHERS WHERE THEY ARE. For feedback to be effective, it's important to tailor the message to meet others where they are. As noted above, this can be related to CQ strength recognition (the introvert and the extrovert, for example). It can also be related to employees' tenure in the workplace and in the organization. For example, you are coaching someone with a few years of work experience and a few months on your team. Your objective is to help the person develop project management skills. Your individual development plan for that person might include a three-month project with a few moving parts as opposed to a one-year strategic plan for the leadership team. Allow the person to learn and grow from where he or she is.

HANDLING UPWARD FEEDBACK. An interesting scenario can occur when, in an organizational context, one person is perceived on paper to have more power than the other—in other words, one is the "boss," and the team member reports to him or her. When there is more of a peer relationship and the boss has demonstrated that input is welcome, upward feedback is a relatively easy conversation. If there are questions about how the lead will receive input and if there may be any unwelcome repercussions for the giver, that's another story. Here are a few tips:

- Work toward having an ongoing healthy relationship with the parties, characterized by constructive conversations.
- Choose a supportive time and place—maybe it's right after your performance review or a meeting with upper management (e.g., both of your bosses).
- Make sure the feedback you offer is practical and as fact-based as possible.
- Consider the other person's communication strengths in determining how direct and to the point you should be.
- Be positive, keep it professional, and focus on opportunities and solutions for the future. As with any feedback conversation:
  - Start with a positive observation.
  - Keep it professional and about the behavior (not about the person).
  - Use questions to ensure it's a give-and-take session.
  - Be prepared to offer specific suggestions for future action.

Note: There may be occasions when *indirection* is a good strategy for upward feedback. For example: "The team has been working on options for how to improve communication with Client X. Would you be interested in hearing some of our ideas?" In this situation, what you're not saying is that the Client X team members have shared with you that they would appreciate your boss submitting progress updates on a more regular basis. Proactive, regular updates happen to be one of the team's recommendations. The hope is, the boss will take a hint on how to improve his or her behavior and better the client relationship.

LANGUAGE EXAMPLES FOR FEEDBACK PROVIDERS. Next are some examples of feedback language to consider on your road to CQ mastery.

Of course, make adjustments based on the communication strengths of the giver and receiver:

INSTEAD OF . . .	YOU COULD TRY . . .
Good job!	Here are three things that you did in the meeting yesterday that had a positive impact on the team (being more specific).
I have a real problem with that.	I see a challenge that we can overcome.
Here's what I think you should do.	Here's what I might do if I were in your position. *or* What would you advise me to do if I were in your position?
That idea doesn't work for me.	That's an interesting approach.
I don't understand your plan.	Can you walk me through your plan?
Why didn't you get back to me sooner?	I want to make sure you received the email. Sometimes technology can mess up.
I don't agree with that approach.	What have you done in the past that achieved good results?

You will notice that the examples in the "You Could Try . . ." column are more positive, more specific, and more inclusive (taking more of a "we" than "me" approach).

For Teams and Organizations

SUPPORT DECENTRALIZED, ONGOING FEEDBACK. We've talked about how the annual review, on its own, does not always achieve intended results. You, as a leader, have the opportunity to set the stage and establish a culture of an ongoing, strengths-oriented process. One important key is to involve everyone early on, ensure the strategy is integrated into daily priorities (versus an additional silo), and check periodically to see what is working and what can be improved. The most important key is that you are personally involved and invested in the process, modeling best practices, and checking in periodically to ensure what you are doing is working and determine how you can improve.

ONBOARD NEW EMPLOYEES GIVING THEM ONGOING FEEDBACK. In addition to annual reviews, many organizations are tied to a one-month or three-month onboarding process before declaring that new employees are ready to fly on their own. Research by Glassdoor finds that a good onboarding process can increase new hire retention by 82 percent and productivity by 70 percent. That's impressive, right? And only 12 percent of employers say their company does a great job at onboarding. For best results, consider onboarding for many positions to be at least a six-month process that includes ongoing feedback.

DO A "STAYING INTERVIEW" (VERSUS EXIT INTERVIEW). This one builds on the principle of you get what you monitor and measure. Who determined that a good *retention* strategy is to conduct an exit interview to assess why someone is leaving? Doesn't it make more sense to determine why valued and high-performing employees are staying? Isn't that the behavior that you want to encourage? Try paying attention to why high performers are staying instead of leaving.

RECOGNIZE CULTURAL DIFFERENCES. A client in an international consulting firm noted that his company was having trouble with employees who either were too aggressive and direct in providing feedback or were hesitant and shy about communicating. It only took a question or two to determine that the more direct providers were from Germany and the holders-back were from Japan. There is a lot of research on cultural differences. Please be aware of this very important factor related to giving and receiving feedback.

PLAN FOR VIRTUAL FEEDBACK. It's a virtual world, and we're living in it. Being engaged in an online or hybrid workspace impacts how feedback is received. (Later in our CQ journey, Chapter 16 is devoted to leveraging virtual.) The primary suggestion is that feedback can be even more important when online is involved. You will likely invest more time in planning, scheduling, and checking in when employees are not with you in person. In a hybrid situation, you will need to ensure you are providing fair and equitable feedback to those who work virtually as well as face-to-face.

ON THE ROAD TO CQ MASTERY— RECEIVING AND GIVING ONGOING FEEDBACK

What have been your experiences in the past with receiving and giving feed-back? Are there occasions in the upcoming week when you have opportu-nities to receive or give feedback? Select two or three strategies from this chapter to apply during those feedback sessions.

CQ TIP. Work through the scenarios and probable outcomes in advance with you're accountability partner. It will help build your confidence and prepare you to apply your CQ!

WHAT'S NEXT?

The next chapter is on one of the most impactful CQ tools—asking effective questions.

CHAPTER
14

CQ7: GOT QUESTIONS?

The answers you receive depend
on the questions you ask, don't they?

If you had an hour to solve a problem, how much time would you invest in framing the question? That was a query considered by Albert Einstein, widely viewed as the most influential scientist of the twentieth century. His answer was, "If I had an hour to solve a problem and my life depended on the solution, I would spend the first 55 minutes determining the proper question to ask, for once I know the proper question, I could solve the problem in less than five minutes." Einstein's 55:5-minute formula may not be the ideal ratio for all situations, but his analysis does shine a light on the importance of questions for Communication Intelligence.

Young children and Einstein have a common tendency to ask questions. Based on your experience and observation, do kids inquire more frequently than adults? Think about it for a minute—how many times have you heard a little voice ask, "Why?"

Research shows that a four-year-old asks an average of 100 questions a day. For an eight-year-old who is in school, the number drops below 50;

189

and by the time the child grows into a working adult in his or her forties, the number drops to below 10.

A primary reason that we ask fewer questions as we grow older is the amount of encouragement we receive. The four-year-old may be fortunate enough to be around parents or guardians who listen and respond to the child's curiosities. The eight-year-old is probably in school, and, you may think, that's where questioning certainly is supported and even taught. After all, we've seen pictures of young students sitting in a classroom with hands raised waiting for the teacher to call on them. However, their hands are usually not raised to answer questions. They are traditionally waiting to answer them, and give the right answer as defined by the teacher.

WHERE ARE YOU NOW?

What is your current level of proficiency regarding asking really good questions?

LEVEL	DESCRIPTORS	WHERE I AM NOW
Novice	I ask questions in the course of communicating and don't give it much thought.	
Intermediate	I regularly ask questions in conversations and in writing that result in the answers I am looking for.	
Mastery	I ask questions that make others think in new ways and that promote good relationships, teamwork, and innovation.	

In this chapter you will:

- Appreciate the *value of good questioning.*
- Identify the relationship between *asking effective questions and communication strengths.*
- Learn about *different types of questions.*
- Develop a personalized *CQ Questioning Plan.*

WHAT ABOUT QUESTIONS IN THE WORKPLACE?

The answers you receive depend on the questions you ask.

It would be nice to think we adults ask fewer questions because, after living for a number of decades, we have all the answers, don't we? The reality is that many workplaces don't encourage inquiry. Frequently, it has to do with how people perceive a question based on their communication style strengths and an organization's culture. The following are some critical knowledge points to be aware of as you expand your skill set here:

- Questions may be viewed as a sign of weakness or lack of ability to perform a task. ("You mean you don't know the answer?")
- Questions may be viewed as challenging authority. ("I can't believe you have the nerve to ask me.")
- In a "Get it done yesterday" and "Time is money" environment, questions may be viewed as holding up progress and slowing down the pace of work.

Are Questions Valuable at Work?

Asking good questions in a work context is essential to frame a purpose and idea, understand the job or task, and build associations with others. Asking good questions is a way to learn and grow, whether you are working for an organization or are self-employed, and regardless of your job title. The answers to the right questions can help you perform more effectively, accomplish goals, and create more enjoyment.

Here are a few examples of the value of questions at work.

SPARK CREATIVITY AND INNOVATION. Questions are the source of knowledge. Most inventions began with a thought-provoking query. The Wright brothers, who invented the airplane, asked, "What if man could fly?" Steve Jobs, CEO of Apple, asked, "Why do phones connect with places and not people?" Maria Telkes, who invented the first fully solar-powered house, asked, "How can the sun be used to heat a home?" Because of these specific questions, fueled by the questioners' curiosity, we have a lot of fantastic inventions today that have shaped our modern world.

Think about a time when you were in a conversation or a meeting and a colleague asked something that energized the room, made you think in a new way, and resulted in the formation of an idea that was worth exploring. That's when questions, in the words of Dan Rothstein, founder of the not-for-profit Right Question Institute, "shine a light on where you need to go."

BUILD RELATIONSHIPS. Asking in order to learn about or from someone else is how you get to know people. On a team, when members ask questions, it's a sign that they are comfortable and in a high-performing environment that encourages openness. People generally appreciate being asked in a way that invites them to share their ideas, knowledge, or expertise.

ADVANCE GOALS AND OBJECTIVES. There are more practical reasons why questions are valuable in a work environment. They are necessary to make sure people are on the same page regarding goals and objectives or, if they are not, to get back on track. Questions are the vehicle to exchange information needed for progress. The next time you are in a work conversation— in person or virtually—observe the role questions play in advancing the agenda (or not). What would be the value of the conversation if nothing were asked?

DO MY COMMUNICATION STRENGTHS INFLUENCE HOW I ASK QUESTIONS?

Yes, yes, and yes.

Your communication strengths influence how you ask questions and how you answer them. Here are some tendencies associated with communication strengths.

PRIMARY STRENGTH	QUESTIONING TENDENCIES
Dominance	Is curious and inquisitive
	Asks direct questions
	Is uncomfortable with indecisive answers
	Can come across as aggressive or critical
Non-Dominance	Appreciates input from others before making a decision
	May hold back from asking questions, even if he or she has unclear or inaccurate information
Extroversion	Asks questions to persuade or control
	May be the first to ask/jump in with a question
	Asks questions to put others at ease
Introversion	Most comfortable asking questions with those he or she knows well
	Thinks through a question before asking
	Is very sincere in his or her questioning approach
Ambiversion	May switch between extroversion and introversion
Patience	Likes time to think through questions and answers
	Is sensitive to those around when framing a question
	Is a good listener
	Is comfortable with positive questions—and less comfortable with questions that create discord or conflict
Impatience	Asks questions to move ahead or speed up action
	Expects others to respond quickly to questions
	May answer a question before it is finished
Conformity	Asks questions to thoroughly understand an environment or situation, or to double-check an answer
	May appreciate asking and answering questions in writing
Non-Conformity	Asks candid questions
	May skip asking a question (assumes the answers)

You may already be thinking about adapting your behavior to be more effective at asking. As additional background, read through the information below on types of questions and tips for effective questioning, and then we'll return to your specific examples and opportunities.

Are There Different Types of Questions?

You've probably heard the saying that "there are no stupid questions." This is generally offered to make people believe that what they are asking is important and worthy of a response. Well, maybe there aren't stupid questions exactly, but there are those that are inappropriate, are uninformed, or have less than positive intentions. Like other communication derailers, these can stop a conversation, create a negative atmosphere, and negatively impact business progress and outcomes.

A sign of communication intelligence is knowing the *right question* to ask at the *right time* to *the right person* and with the *right intent*. Most queries can be broken down into one of four categories: empowering questions, closed-ended and open-ended questions, practical questions, and rhetorical questions. Let's look at those now:

- **EMPOWERING QUESTIONS.** An empowering question is one that makes the other person think in a new way. It can inspire creative thought and outside-the-box answers. This type should be tailored to an individual or situation. The answer should *not* be something that you can easily find on the internet. Salespeople, for example, can use power questions to uncover needs that prospects didn't even know they had. A consultant can use them to bring a client to value a new solution. A leader can use them to inspire and motivate team members to grow through a challenging time. Examples include:
    - When you wake up tomorrow, what would make you excited about going to work?
    - How have you and your team been so successful at earning loyalty from your clients?
    - What lessons are we learning from yesterday that make us proud of what we stand for as a team?
- **CLOSED-ENDED AND OPEN-ENDED QUESTIONS.** You have probably heard of this classification. Closed-ended questions lead to a yes or no response or a choice from a select number of options (e.g., a multiple-choice format). Open-ended questions invite a broader answer and explanation. When might you use each type?

- Closed-ended questions may be useful when you are collecting data. They may make sense when you want to know facts and trends, or want to determine whether there is a clear consensus among a group or team. They tend to start with "did," "have," "will," or "can."
- Open-ended questions are more appropriate when you want to elicit thoughts, ideas, or feelings or encourage brainstorming. They likely start with "how," "why," or "what if."

A sign of CQ is being able to determine the right option for a specific situation. For example, if someone is in a job interview, which one of these questions would help determine whether the candidate is a good match for the position?

- **Closed-ended.** Have you ever been in a position when you had to communicate negative news to a customer? Yes or no?
- **Open-ended.** Can you tell me about a time when you had to communicate negative news to a customer? What happened next?

- **PRACTICAL QUESTIONS.** These tend to be "what," "when," and "where" questions. They are asked in order to find information needed to accomplish a task in a correct, timely, and appropriate manner. For example, at a project status meeting, questions to be answered might include:
  - What are the materials we need to accomplish the next task?
  - When is the next deadline?
  - Where is the next meeting?
- **RHETORICAL QUESTIONS.** These are the questions that don't really require an answer—they restate something that is known or obvious. In their best form, they can be used to ensure agreement or to engage in friendly conversation. For example:
  - Isn't the weather beautiful today?
  - Wasn't the last presentation informative?
  - Don't you like working with our new team member?

QUESTIONING TIPS

FRAME THE RIGHT QUESTION. What is the answer you're looking for? The reason Einstein invested 55 minutes of an hour framing the right question is that *the answer you receive depends on what you ask.* Let's say you are at a client discovery meeting and the team leader has laid out the plan in great detail. At the end, the leader asks, "Any questions?" Here are three that might come to mind:

- What will be the value of the project to the client and its customers?
- Are you sure we have the materials in stock to do the project?
- What if we don't meet the deadline?

Each of these questions has pros and cons depending on the environment and the people in the room. This is very situational, and done properly it demonstrates your listening skills. Make sure your questions move the moment forward!

KNOW YOUR COMMUNICATION STRENGTHS. When you have formulated what you believe is the right question, what is your tendency in how and when you ask it? A key is to understand your communication strength, how others are likely to perceive you and the question, and how to adapt to be more effective and to obtain the answers that you want. This also means understanding your communication strengths related to follow-up questions.

UNDERSTAND OTHERS' QUESTIONING STRENGTHS. Even if those in the room don't have labels that read "Primary Strength: Non-Conformist" or "Primary Strength: Patience," you should be able to determine general strengths. When you understand a person's strength, you can use that to motivate you to adapt.

BE POSITIVE. There are few things more destructive than a negatively worded question. As emphasized earlier, there are numerous advantages to positivity. To use positive or negative wording, for most people, is a choice with tremendous influence on the work environment. Positivity correlates with improved business outcomes, including employee engagement, retention, productivity, and safety. The distinction can be particularly prominent among leaders. According to the Gallup research organization, disengaged management and employees in the United States cost between $960 billion and $1.2 trillion per year. Globally, the cost is almost $7 trillion, which amounts to 9 to 10 percent of the world's gross domestic product.

Even if you are delivering a negative message, you can frame a question positively. For example, let's say a new hire is struggling to implement a procedure, and you are asked to be a mentor. You can ask:

- "Are you just not up to the job?"
- Or, "I know you have what it takes to accomplish this task. May I work with you on the next step?"

The first question will likely lead to defensiveness, a greater lack of confidence, and confusion on the part of the employee. The second option will bring relief, prompt a willingness to take constructive action, and build rapport.

LISTEN ALL THE WAY THROUGH THE ANSWER. Regardless of your communication strengths, it is important to listen all the way through the answer to the question you have asked. If the answer is not worth listening to, then maybe you didn't ask the best question. And then say thank you, to acknowledge the time and thought that went into the response even if you don't initially like or understand the answer.

CQ QUESTIONING PLAN STRATEGY

Creating a CQ Questioning Plan can be very helpful in organizing your thoughts and feelings. The following table shows an example of a CQ Questioning Plan for someone with the primary strength of patience.

SITUATION OR TASK	TENDENCY	RESULT	ADAPTED BEHAVIOR	RESULT
Tomorrow's meeting on how to respond to customer feedback	To hold back and not ask questions. Even though I have researched this thoroughly and know the data we need to have. I'm nervous even thinking about it.	The meeting won't achieve the intended result. I will feel like I let the team down. John (team lead) will wonder why I didn't speak up. Everyone will be even more frustrated.	I can prepare a few questions, practice them, and be more comfortable. I will pay attention to when there is an opportunity to ask—at least within the first quarter of the time. I will contribute by asking the needed questions.	People may be surprised (in a good way?) that I asked. Customers will benefit. We may earn more repeat business. Morale will improve. I will be happier!

Now it's your turn to make a plan. Use the answers to these questions to help you complete the next table.

- What is your primary strength?
- What is a situation or task coming up that will involve your asking questions?
- What is your tendency in the situation?
- What are the likely results if you act on your tendency?
- How will you adapt your behavior?
- What will be the adapted results?

SITUATION OR TASK	TENDENCY	RESULT	ADAPTED BEHAVIOR	RESULT

What actually happened, and what are the results so far?

_____

_____

_____

_____

ON THE ROAD TO CQ MASTERY—GOT QUESTIONS?

In addition to applying the CQ Questioning Plan, here are a few suggestions to help build your CQ in this area:

- Observe questions today. When and why are you asking questions? What questions are others asking? Are questions advancing or impeding a goal or objective?
- How does your communication strength impact your questioning? What happens as you adapt?
- What do you think of the culture of inquiry in your workplace?
- How do questions impact your relationships and communication— whether in person, virtually, or through email?
- Have a conversation with your accountability partner.

Any questions?

WHAT'S NEXT?

The next chapter is on one of the most valuable and least understood aspects of CQ—non-verbal communication.

CHAPTER 15

CQ8: CRYSTALLIZING NON-VERBAL COMMUNICATION

*When your words and non-verbal signals align,
your CQ crystallizes and builds trust
and confidence in you and your message.*

The road to mastery of CQ8—non-verbal communication—begins with *awareness*. Many people don't realize the significance of non-verbal cues (these cues are the majority of how we communicate) and the disconnect between what they say through their actions and how it is received. Let's listen in on two sales presentations to help understand how reading non-verbal communication is a CQ game changer.

SCENARIO 1: THE SALES PRESENTATION
AND NON-VERBAL AFFIRMATION

The in-person sales presentation is set for an hour, and your team of three is right on time. After weeks of preparation, the pitch starts as planned. During the session, you observe the people on the prospect's leadership team (the decision makers are in the room) as they listen and ask pertinent questions. They share approving nods, and most lean forward, making eye contact with you and your team. To conclude the session, the CEO says, "Thank you. You'll have our decision tomorrow." He rises to shake your hand. The tone of his voice, the lifted eyebrows, and the smile speak volumes. You bet that your team earned the sale.

SCENARIO 2: THE SALES PRESENTATION
AND NON-VERBAL CANCELLATION

The hour-long sales presentation is drawing to a close, and your heart is beating fast. From the beginning, the CEO has sat back in her chair with arms crossed. She darts seemingly annoyed glances at her colleagues and repeatedly checks her watch. As the meeting draws to a close, she stands up, crosses her hands over her chest again, and says in a nondescript, low voice, "Thank you. You'll have our decision tomorrow." Your confidence level, to say the least, is not high.

The CEO in both scenarios concludes with the same exact words: "Thank you. You'll have our decision tomorrow"—but their meanings are worlds apart. The question for you is, how proficient was your CQ at deciphering the true meaning? What about the cues in the meetings leading up to the final presentation? Was your team equipped to interpret and translate the volume of non-verbal intelligence that was offered?

Non-verbal communication is the secret sauce of CQ. When you are able to decode the cues, you are positioned to be a more consistent communicator and miles ahead of most of the competition when it comes to understanding others. When you are able to adapt your non-verbal communication to align with your words and intentions, you are closer to mastering CQ.

WHERE ARE YOU NOW?

Where is your current level of proficiency related to non-verbal communication?

LEVEL	DESCRIPTION	WHERE I AM NOW
Novice	I haven't thought about non-verbal communication. I can sense that something is not quite right in how others communicate, but I'm not sure how to explain why.	
Intermediate	I'm aware that there's an impact of non-verbal communication and that words and body language can contradict each other. I've started to be aware of my non-verbal cues.	
Mastery	I am able to interpret the non-verbal signals of others. I adapt my non-verbal behavior to align with my words. I receive the feedback I want as I align my words, intentions, and non-verbal communication.	

In this chapter, you will:

- Appreciate why understanding *non-verbal communication is the secret sauce* of CQ.
- Identify *eight areas of non-verbal communication.*
- Explore if *you are articulate* (e.g., coherent and fluent) in non-verbal communication.
- Document *steps* you can take to *crystallize non-verbal communication.*

ACCOUNTABILITY PARTNER NOTE. Non-verbal communication is a fascinating and eye-opening journey. This is an area where you and your accountability partner can help each other and have fun in the process.

WHAT IS NON-VERBAL COMMUNICATION?

Non-verbal communication is the foundation for how we interact with others. It refers to the way we give and receive information, emotions, and messages beyond words. The advanced understanding of non-verbal communication dates to 1872 and Charles Darwin (you know him in terms of Darwinism and his theory of evolution). In his publication, *The Expressions of the Emotions of Man and Animals*, he shared his observations that animals—e.g., dogs, lions, tigers—communicate through expressions and gestures. (I don't know about you, but I know for certain that the dogs and cats I have been privileged to know have mastered the art of communicating non-verbally.)

Non-Verbal Is How We Communicate Most of the Time

In considering the ways we communicate—words, gestures—what percentage would you say is non-verbal? There are a variety of studies that conclude that non-verbal is the vast majority of how we message, in the range of 70 to 93 percent. Experts also agree that spoken words account for a minority of the ways communication is understood (compared, for example, with body language, facial expressions, and the tone of your voice). However, there are a variety of factors that influence how to accurately interpret specific interactions—we'll dive into these in a minute.

If you've never considered the impact of this dominant force, this is a potentially important moment in your CQ evolution. Think about it—those who take for granted, ignore, or misinterpret non-verbal communication are potentially missing the whole ball game.

Consider how non-verbal communication impacts various professions:

- **SALESPEOPLE.** They are able to interpret whether a prospect is more or less inclined to buy through understanding non-verbal behavior.
- **RESTAURANT SERVERS.** Non-verbal communication sets the stage for whether a customer has a good experience (is there good eye

contact, friendly facial expressions, appropriate proximity?) . . . or not.

- **COUNSELORS AND THERAPISTS.** They glean information about how a client is actually feeling and thinking, in ways that the client may not even understand—e.g., is a couple saying they're getting along when they aren't looking at each other and their feet are pointed in opposite directions?
- **LAWYERS.** They are able to analyze the extent to which someone is telling the truth and guide clients on how their body language may influence a jury's deliberations.
- **LAW ENFORCEMENT.** It's critical to focus on their own and the body language of those they encounter every day in every way, from a routine traffic stop to an emergency intervention.
- **NEGOTIATORS.** They could be closing a deal for a merger of companies and benefit from interpreting whether an agreement is near or not. On the international stage, world leaders may be negotiating whether a conflict turns into all-out war, and expert interpretation of non-verbal communication could be a key component in the outcome. (There's a reason that the US government has spent millions of dollars studying the body language of primary world figures such as Russian president Vladmir Putin. And that some other nations do the same.)

What is the influence of non-verbal communication in your line of work and in your position? Understanding the answer to this question could help you to:

- Prevent miscommunication and conflict
- Save time and energy
- Build credibility
- Feel more confident and engaged

HOW OFTEN SHOULD YOU BE AWARE OF YOUR NON-VERBAL COMMUNICATION AT WORK? (*HINT:* SOMEBODY IS PROBABLY WATCHING)

Researchers at Yale University conducted a study in which they asked employees to observe their boss walking from the parking lot to the front door of the office in the morning before the workday had begun. A criterion was that the employees had to have worked for their leader for at least six months—in other words, they had a baseline for observing his behavior. After assessing his body language during the 20-second walk, employees were able to accurately predict the kind of day they would have. For example, if the boss approached the door with his head down and shaking his head negatively, there might be a rough shift ahead. The point is that there is a good chance that others are checking out your non-verbal behavior at work even if you are not aware of it.

How long does it take for others to solidify their impression of you? Research shows that it could take as little as a tenth of a second to lock in some aspects (e.g., "Do I trust this person?") and seven seconds to cement a point of view. This is likely long before you've shared any verbal information about yourself or your company or any information related to any business agenda.

There may have been occasions when you've reached a conclusion about someone quite a while before a formal introduction. For example, a new person appears in the workspace on a tour. You observe that she has a calm demeanor, nods her head a lot, appears to be a good listener, and you like the way she is professionally dressed. A few days later, you notice this person in the conference room, and although you can't hear the conversation, her intent listening posture and the handshake concluding the session have your non-verbal antenna on alert. Sure enough, you find out the next week that the mystery woman is your new boss. The impression is set that you'll probably get along with her before a word has been spoken.

Others may be watching you at any time—or most times—during a workday if you are in a physical workspace. Particularly if you are in a leadership position, you can safely assume that those you work with are looking for opportunities to check out your non-verbal signals all the time. The best advice is to be self-aware and be your best non-verbal self at all times.

HOW DO YOU COMMUNICATE NON-VERBALLY? As with other aspects of CQ, the road to mastery begins with self-awareness. For the next 24 hours, simply recognize when and how you are communicating non-verbally. Start to become aware of how others respond to your cues.

BREAKING IT DOWN—EIGHT FORMS OF NON-VERBAL COMMUNICATION

There are myriad aspects of non-verbal communication ranging from the obvious to the more subtle and from the intentional to the less conscious. In the next table you'll find eight forms of non-verbal communication that will help guide you on the road to more awareness in terms of yourself and others. As you review the categories in the table, notice the "Focus" column. You are invited to use it to select the top two or three areas that could positively impact the effectiveness of communication at work.

Here are a few considerations to keep in mind as you review the table:

- *These are examples to get you started.* You may come up with more of your own based on your experience and as your awareness grows.
- As with all aspects of communication, *your personal strengths impact non-verbal messaging.* If your primary strength is extroversion, do you have a tendency to gesture more frequently with your hands while speaking? With a primary strength of impatience, do you hold eye contact for a longer or shorter period of time?

- *Beware of jumping to a conclusion based on a single non-verbal indicator.* That means that no single sign or expression should be interpreted without considering context and a more holistic view of the situation and what is being communicated. For example, here are a few indications that someone may be less than truthful in what he or she is saying:
  - Blinking eyes more quickly than usual or not at all
  - Maintaining eye contact more intensely or avoiding eye contact
  - Pressing lips together
  - Tapping feet or moving legs restlessly
  - Fidgeting

  There might be alternative explanations for any one of these. Someone may be blinking her eyes because of an irritation or too much sunlight instead of trying to deceive. Someone may be tapping his foot because his primary strength is dominance. However, when a cluster or combination of these behaviors is present, it may be more likely that the person is being deceptive.

- *There are documented cultural differences* that impact non-verbal communication. Be aware of these, and conduct additional research into areas that are relevant to your work situation. For example, people from Peru and Argentina find it normal to stand closer to others than those from Hungary. Japanese people tend to maintain neutral facial expressions compared with their Western counterparts. Cultures in Asia and the Middle East can interpret direct eye contact as offensive.

- *If you know colleagues well,* you probably have a baseline of their non-verbal cues and are in a position to determine if they are deviating from their norm. To reiterate, non-verbal communication conveys emotions that can provide insights more accurately than words. For example, you are at work and a colleague who is normally positively inclined arrives at a meeting late, shoves her briefcase under the table, and slumps into a chair. You ask (somewhat concerned), "Are you OK?" She responds, "I'm just fine." In this case, which do you believe are more reliable indicators of what's she's experiencing: her words or her body language?

As mentioned, the following table offers eight forms of non-verbal communication for your consideration. As you read through the table, feel free to select two or three to focus on by checking the "Focus" column on the right.

NON-VERBAL COMMUNICATION DESCRIPTION (EXAMPLES)	WHAT THE DESCRIPTIONS MEAN (EXAMPLES)	FOCUS AREAS (Choose two to three)
Posture. This refers to the way you stand, sit, and use your hands in relation to your body. There are two basic types of posture—open and closed.	Your posture relates to your confidence level. It can reveal emotions and intentions such as whether you are receptive (or not) to what is being conveyed. **Open posture.** This is when hands are open and arms are uncrossed. This conveys that someone is interested in what he or she is hearing or seeing. **Closed posture.** This involves legs crossed, arms folded, and shoulders slumped. This generally indicates someone is not interested, is distracted, or is uncomfortable.	
Facial expressions. Depending on their communication strengths and cultural orientation, people can have a tendency to be more or less emotionally controlled, which influences their facial expressions. "His face is an open book" may be at one extreme and "poker face" at the other. Examples include the position of your mouth—e.g., is there a smile or a frown? Are eyebrows raised or lowered?	Smiles (when they are genuine) indicate happiness or a positive mood. Frowns mean lack of concentration, displeasure, or worry. Raised eyebrows can indicate welcome, surprise, and openness. They also can indicate disbelief or doubt. Lowered eyebrows can indicate a feeling of concern or the questioning of a message or authority. *Here's an exercise:* Try to smile and lower your eyebrows at the same time. Then try to raise your eyebrows and frown at the same time. Look in the mirror. A bit awkward, isn't it?	

(continued on next page)

NON-VERBAL COMMUNICATION DESCRIPTION (EXAMPLES)	WHAT THE DESCRIPTIONS MEAN (EXAMPLES)	FOCUS AREAS (Choose two to three)
Eyes. Are your eyes, as the well-known saying goes, truly "the windows to your soul"? Eye cues are one of the most obvious ways that you communicate. They certainly do express volumes through, for example, the intensity of eye contact (looking directly or away) or the amount that they are open or closed (e.g., surprised eyes, glaring eyes, rolling eyes).	*Looking at someone directly* for a long time can be interpreted as threatening, superiority, or a lack of respect. *Not maintaining eye contact* can be a sign of shyness, insecurity, or low interest. *Maintaining positive eye contact* generally indicates that feedback is being well received. *Rolling of eyes*, for most, has a negative connotation, indicating someone doesn't believe or trust what another person is saying. *Tips:* A good rule of thumb is to maintain eye contact about 60% of the time with an interested intent. Another good rule is to match the manner of the person you're communicating with in a positive interaction.	
Gestures. Most gestures involve the hands and arms. These can include pointing, waving, shaking hands with someone, and rubbing hands or palms together. There are also more subtle gestures such as tilting your head, touching your earlobes, stroking your chin, or rubbing your eyes.	People who tend to "talk with their hands" are perceived to be more energetic, friendly, and agreeable. Those who use less gesturing are viewed as more analytical and logical.	

NON-VERBAL COMMUNICATION DESCRIPTION (EXAMPLES)	WHAT THE DESCRIPTIONS MEAN (EXAMPLES)	FOCUS AREAS (Choose two to three)
Voice. Your voice—the pitch, tone, volume, speed, and emphasis—has an enormous impact on how your message is received, particularly if you are communicating on the phone. For example, you can "hear" a smile. Many companies pay rapt attention and invest in the "tone of voice" conveyed in written and spoken communication that reflects their brand.	**PITCH** **Higher pitch.** When you hear a voice rise at the end of a sentence, it generally indicates that the speaker is asking a question. It also may indicate that someone is nervous or unsure of what he or she is saying. A higher pitch and quicker speed can indicate enthusiasm. **Lower pitch.** It can project authority. Or a lower pitch and slower speed can indicate "I want to be left alone." **TONE** There are many ways to think of tone. You can think of tone as conveying an attitude or setting a scene: Humorous or serious (professional) Informal or formal Motivating or cautionary Assertive or passive Respectful or dismissive Familiar or distant You can think of tone as conveying emotion: **Angry tone.** Obviously, it conveys anger or frustration. **Happy tone.** It's upbeat and positive. What was your tone in a recent conversation? **SPEED** Faster talking can mean someone is enthusiastic. "Fast talk" can also be interpreted as clever or suspicious. As a general rule, moderately slower is better in order to be heard and understood.	

(continued on next page)

NON-VERBAL COMMUNICATION DESCRIPTION (EXAMPLES)	WHAT THE DESCRIPTIONS MEAN (EXAMPLES)	FOCUS AREAS (Choose two to three)
Proximity and personal space. This refers to the amount of space that is created or allowed between individuals. There are strong cultural influences on the amount of personal space—for example, there are higher-contact and lower-contact cultures.	*Higher-contact cultures* tend to stand closer, speak louder, and touch more frequently. Examples include those from South America, the Middle East, and Southern European countries. *Lower-contact cultures* tend to maintain greater interpersonal distance and have less face-to-face positioning. Paying attention to proximity in the workplace is particularly important because the "right" distance, as are other aspects of interaction, is about perception. If distance is perceived as too close or "invading someone's space," someone can be uncomfortable or feel demeaned. This can be perceived as harassment, which requires referring to HR protocols as appropriate. *Tip:* For work, a guideline is to maintain a social distance that is generally viewed as being four to twelve feet apart (compared with a personal distance, which is two to four feet apart).	
Physical reactions. These can include blushing, sweating, teary eyes, clammy handshakes, and sighing. These physiological changes are not always in your control. They are part of how you communicate non-verbally.	These types of physical reactions generally communicate that someone is uncomfortable, has been caught off guard, or is ill at ease. *Tips: If you find yourself experiencing these types of reactions,* efforts such as taking deep breaths and focusing on the present (instead of what your mind might be worrying about) can be helpful. You might also take a break to regroup and regain composure. *When you recognize these cues in others,* you can be proactive in reassuring them, making them feel more comfortable, or giving them a break to recompose.	

NON-VERBAL COMMUNICATION DESCRIPTION (EXAMPLES)	WHAT THE DESCRIPTIONS MEAN (EXAMPLES)	FOCUS AREAS (Choose two to three)
Dress and décor. The way you choose to dress and groom communicates your personal style and beliefs. How you choose to decorate your workspace conveys your interests and priorities. In a virtual environment, the background or screen picture can have significance.	*Consider the messaging* you convey through the eyes of others. For example: The knapsack you are sporting may remind you of that gap year in Central America, but is it appropriate for a meeting with a client when the business wants to establish a professional brand? In your view, a bow tie may signal your uniqueness on casual Friday. How is it being perceived by others? Is that T-shirt appropriate for your new position in the golf resort gift shop that requires members to wear shirts with collars? *Tip*: It's a good practice to consider the formality of the event or occasion when choosing what you communicate through your dress and décor. Check dress codes and options for your position and company, if available. Ask others for their views on this aspect of your non-verbal communication.	

ARE YOU ARTICULATE IN NON-VERBAL COMMUNICATION?

A goal in crystallizing non-verbal communication is to have the intention of your words align with that of your non-verbal signals. Are you coherent and fluent in this arena?

Look at Take 1 below and ask yourself, "Are the two parties aligned in their messaging?"

First Day Learning Session, Take 1

SITUATION. Giovanni, the team lead, is providing instructions to Ariel, a new call center associate on her first day of work, on how to conduct a cold call.

ACTION. Giovanni's gaze canvases the room as he demonstrates the procedures for Ariel. Ariel follows his moves, looking for eye contact so she can check for understanding. Giovanni is distracted by an animated conversation nearby and ends the training session by glancing at Ariel and asking if she understands his instructions. Ariel slowly says yes as her head shakes hesitatingly side to side, signaling she is not at all confident. "Good," says Giovanni, "I'll check in with you later." Ariel proceeds to ask George (who has worked there for six years and has his own way of conducting a call) for guidance, which she follows since she wasn't clear about what her team lead was saying.

RESULT. Later in the day, Giovanni checks in with Ariel and sees that she is not performing according to his direction. Then comes her first write-up and warning as her first day on the job comes to a close.

Did Giovanni's intention, words, and non-verbal communication align? They did not. He didn't have appropriate eye contact. He was clearly focused on activity other than connecting with Ariel. And he failed to read Ariel's body language as she communicated with her side-to-side head movement that she didn't understand.

Ariel tried to capture Giovanni's attention through eye contact during the training session. When she had a chance to ask for clarification, her words said, "I understand," while her body language didn't align. The result wasn't satisfactory for either party. So let's rewind and try this again.

First Day Learning Session, Take 2

SITUATION. Giovanni, the team lead, is providing instructions to Ariel, a new call center associate on her first day of work, on how to conduct a cold call.

ACTION. Giovanni explains his objectives for the session as he maintains positive eye contact with Ariel. He checks in periodically with positive body language to ensure she is understanding what he says, nodding his head in encouragement and affirmation. At the conclusion of his demonstration, he asks what's on Ariel's mind with raised eyebrows, a smile, and a palm-side-up hand gesture.

Ariel asks for clarification with slightly wider eyes and a professional posture. She nods her head affirmatively as her team lead repeats the procedure, checking in to ensure understanding. "I've got this," Ariel concludes with a smile. Giovanni signals an OK sign and says he'll check in with her later.

RESULT. Later in the day, Giovanni checks in with Ariel. She has had a successful first day on the job and is confident she made a good choice accepting a position with the company. Giovanni's job is now easier, as he has another motivated and competent employee on his team.

The fact that the team lead and the new employee aligned their intended words with their body language, "read" the other's messaging accurately, and adapted made all the difference. The result is a win-win for both parties.

Here are a few more guidelines for your alignment:

- **LOOK FOR INCONSISTENT SIGNALS.** Pay extra attention when verbal and non-verbal messages don't match up in your, or others', communication. For example, misalignment occurs when someone who is saying you have more time to present in a meeting is tapping her pen on the desk. Or when you are saying "You have my full attention" while checking your phone. When words say one thing and body language suggests something else, focus a little more on what the non-verbal cues indicate.

- **ASK QUESTIONS.** If you notice incongruent behavior, a good strategy is to ask questions. As noted in Chapter 14, effective queries lead to clarity. And they can (re)focus the communicator on his intentions. A good strategy is to check for understanding. Some sample phrases:
    - "What I hear you saying is . . ."
    - "May I check for understanding? . . ."
    - "Are you thinking that we should . . .?"

- **USE NON-VERBAL GESTURES TO EMPHASIZE AND ADD MEANING.** As you become more proficient in non-verbal CQ, you will become more comfortable and effective with aligning gestures to add meaning. For example, if you are giving a presentation, you can "read the room" for receptivity and adapt hand gestures and eye contact to emphasize key points. You can reinforce that you are confident and prepared by standing or sitting with a straight and balanced posture.

- **AVOID EXAGGERATION.** It can be tempting as you are learning the CQ non-verbal ropes to exaggerate non-verbal messaging or to overemphasize. You've seen the person with an overbroad smile and eyes darting back and forth who comes across as a comedian. Or the person in a meeting (in person or virtual) with head down and eyebrows lowered to an extreme, shaking his head widely from side to side trying to signal he doesn't agree with what is being said. *Subtlety* can be more effective than exaggeration in most cases.

- **PRACTICE!** Like most skills, mastering non-verbal CQ will come more easily to some than others. The good news is that you can improve with attention and practice. Try it out by rehearsing in front of a mirror, by taking a video, or by asking someone for feedback. The more comfortable you get, the more non-verbal will seamlessly align with your words, and you will be one of the few in the CQ Non-Verbal Mastery Club.

ON THE ROAD TO CQ MASTERY— CRYSTALLIZING NON-VERBAL COMMUNICATION

GENERAL AWARENESS. Here are a few ideas to build general awareness:

- The next time you visit a coffee shop, restaurant, or other venue where people are interacting, observe their non-verbal communication. What do you believe they are experiencing?
- Turn on a favorite TV show or movie, and turn down the sound. What do you believe the people are communicating?
- Invest time at work observing non-verbal behaviors in the office. What is really going on behind the window of the meeting room? What is being communicated in the break room?

SELF-AWARENESS. Here are a few ideas to build awareness of your non-verbal tendencies:

- Identify non-verbal preferences you have tied to your communication strengths.

- Monitor at a next meeting or interaction how you communicate non-verbally and how it is received.
- Choose to be more intentional (for example, in one or more of the eight non-verbal types described earlier).

AWARENESS OF OTHERS. Here is an idea to build awareness of others:

- Apply what you have learned in your next meeting or interaction to others' non-verbal communication. Invest time to look at clusters of messaging instead of jumping to a conclusion based on one gesture or eye movement.

ADVANCED AWARENESS. And here are a couple of ideas to build advanced awareness:

- Build team non-verbal communication skills. Share what you have learned with others on your team. Establish a plan to enhance awareness and application.
- Be sensitive to the cultural impacts on non-verbal communication. You may be interacting with other cultures or curious about cultural differences. For example, you may serve one team in Japan and one in Germany, and there are occasions when the two interact in a virtual meeting. Research the ways each culture relays non-verbal messages and their meanings.

WHAT'S NEXT?

If you haven't been working in a virtual or hybrid space, chances are you will at some point. The next chapter is on how communication is the number one skill needed to be effective in these brave newer worlds.

CHAPTER
16

CQ9: CONNECTING THROUGH VIRTUAL COMMUNICATION

What are the top skills employees need
to succeed in the virtual workspace?
Communication and adaptability.

There is a plethora of videos on the internet that are parodies of communication in the virtual workspace. One features Jerome, who has a tendency to dominate conversations, while Anna is the introvert, who is more comfortable with the chat feature than trying to compete with others. A participant can't figure out how to unmute, and others have their video turned off. Then there's the team member whose technology is having a bad day and keeps disconnecting. More than a few are playing the pretending-to-be-engaged game—that is, they're actually checking emails, playing a video, or making a list for the kid's birthday party, while nodding and smiling. These videos have millions of views for a reason. Videos help people connect and communicate over common interests, or some are just hilarious! And there is a serious convenience factor—while it is fun to go to a movie theater, you can also do essentially the same thing at home sans having the popcorn prepared for you!

Although there are challenging aspects to the newer frontier of digital communication, the majority of workers and employers who choose virtual options find the medium to be positive in its flexibility, productivity, and cost savings.

Even though there is a lot unknown about what the future holds, one thing that is certain is that virtual is here to stay. Whether you are a long-time telecommuter, have recently been thrust into the remote stratosphere, or have yet to experience this world, chances are that you will be called on to rise to the virtual CQ challenge.

THE NEWER FRONTIER

I was talking with someone the other day who is a respected leader in the financial field. His company, like many others, jumped to an online platform during COVID. Given the nature of the work, the vast majority of the organization's jobs are suited for a virtual environment. The leaders in his company are weighing their policies regarding what's next:

- Will they require employees to return to face-to-face and encourage in-person interaction with customers?
- Will they retain virtual as the primary communication vehicle?
- Will they give flexibility to employees to determine how they will operate in the workspace?

His take on the matter was that it didn't make much difference; communication was all the same except with technology you talk through a screen.

Hmm. That had me wondering how many people are disregarding or underestimating the impact of technology on communication.

WHERE ARE YOU NOW?

Where are you today in your proficiency level of virtual communication?

LEVEL	DESCRIPTORS	WHERE I AM NOW
Novice	I've never been a remote worker. *or* I can use help in connecting and communicating remotely.	
Intermediate	I understand the differences between remote and in-person communication. I attempt to communicate more effectively online.	
Mastery	I exercise patience when it comes to working with others remotely. I take responsibility for how I can adapt to maximize my productivity, and that of the team, in a virtual or hybrid environment.	

THE STATE OF DIGITAL

Remote work isn't new. Those of a certain age may remember the term "telecommuting"—where workers had greater flexibility in their work hours and locations, and which became part of the vernacular in the 1970s. In 1979, IBM gave five employees the ability to telecommute in a pilot study, which was expanded to 2,000 people by 1983. There has been a steady increase in the number of remote workers since then. For example, more than 4 million people joined the virtual ranks between 2004 and 2006.

Then came COVID.

According to government data, about 51 million Americans worked remotely in 2019 (pre-COVID), or almost one-third of the 160 million Americans who were employed that fall. Remote working reached a high in October 2020, during the pandemic, when about 70 percent of those whose jobs were compatible worked from home all or most of the time. This was a revolution (versus an evolution) for most, because almost 60 percent had never or rarely had worked from home prior to the pandemic. Just getting the "home office" up and running was no small feat! Then there was the family in the same space 24/7. For double-income households sharing this new workspace—wow! Yet in so many ways we were blessed with technology, and commerce continued in very new and different ways.

Where Are We Going?

I don't have a crystal ball, but I can say that based on conversations with experts around the world and studying research and surveys on an ongoing basis, virtual and hybrid are here to stay. As the pandemic waned, there was a swing toward more in-person work connections, but the positive aspects of remote have made their mark. First of all, virtual work and virtual education are possible and getting better. As far as virtual work goes, it has caused those daily hour(s)-long commutes to be minimized, corporate travel to be reassessed, and in-office workspace to be reimagined. And the benefits of virtual education? Running between classes for professors and students is minimized, and that easy cup of coffee from the kitchen and other creature comforts are other positives. All this said, it's important to note that a Pew Research Center study found that, even with all the attention on virtual options, most US workers—about 60 percent—don't currently have positions that are compatible with remote options. Overall, though, online platforms are enabling extended teams to more effectively collaborate and communicate in new and exciting ways.

BENEFITS AND CHALLENGES OF REMOTE WORK

The Duarte Group, a thought leader in work communication since 1988, surveyed business professionals on the skills employees need to succeed in virtual and hybrid environments. The findings are that the more that technology is relied on, the more CQ is valued. The top desirable competencies are communication and adaptability.

As mentioned earlier in the book, I founded The Forté Institute in the 1970s with the knowledge that these two empowering skills—communication and adaptability—are essential for success at work and in life.

According to Duarte, the top three challenges for organizations related to CQ are:

- Communicating well in online and virtual settings
- Cascading messages across the organization
- Communicating to achieve and maintain alignment among stakeholders

The survey found that when it comes to achieving a proficient level, there is work to be done, because employees' communication skills were rated at a 6.48 on a 10-point scale.

Although experiences vary from person to person, there are positive aspects of remote workspace options, and there are challenges. Being aware of the advantages can set the stage for having more effective CQ and building robust connections, while being aware that the disadvantages can be CQ derailers may take targeted focus and actions to overcome.

Benefits

Based on your experience, what are the greatest benefits of remote working? Put a check mark in the appropriate boxes in the table. If you are not currently working virtually or haven't yet tapped into the newer frontier, base your answers on current knowledge and observation. Broader explanations of each element are provided in the following table.

COMMUNICATION INTELLIGENCE

BENEFIT	LEVEL OF IMPORTANCE		
	LOWER	MODERATE	STRONG
Flexibility and autonomy—I appreciate having more control of my schedule.			
Work-life balance—I am able to better balance my work and personal life.			
Savings in time and money—I'm saving money.			
Environmental benefits—I appreciate that remote working positively supports the environment versus commuting.			

Here are broader explanations of these benefits:

- **FLEXIBILITY/AUTONOMY.** This is the number one benefit according to multiple polls. Almost 70 percent of workers value having options in how they allocate their time. For many employees, remote workspaces have become more of a supportive structure for the human work experience. With digital meeting rooms, collaboration applications, and other cloud services, team members can choose which type of environment works best for them.
- **WORK-LIFE BALANCE.** The Pew Research Center reports that when it comes to balancing work and personal life, working from home has made it:
    - ○ Easier—64 percent
    - ○ Harder—16 percent
    - ○ About the same—20 percent
- **SAVINGS IN TIME AND MONEY FOR EMPLOYEES.** Since there is no longer a commute, workers save on gas and/or other transportation costs, and they also are not spending as much money on eating out.
- **SAVINGS IN TIME AND MONEY FOR EMPLOYERS AND ORGANIZATIONS.** Travel budgets are significant. So, working remotely saves companies money.
- **ENVIRONMENTAL BENEFITS.** There are also the environmental aspects of fewer commutes. For example, it can help lessen

greenhouse gas emissions attributed to transportation, there is less use of fossil fuels, the carbon footprint is lowered, and there is reduced air pollution.

Challenges

Based on your experience, what are the greatest challenges of remote working? Put a check mark in the appropriate boxes in the table. As with benefits, if you are not currently working virtually or haven't yet tapped into the newer frontier, base your answers on current knowledge and observation. Broader explanations of each element are provided below.

CHALLENGE	LEVEL OF SIGNIFICANCE		
	DISAGREE	AGREE	STRONGLY AGREE
Communication strength differences			
Less face-to-face (not as connected—isolation)			
Less or less effective feedback (e.g., from customers, bosses, team members)			
Pressure to stand out—bias potential			
Distractions at home			
Disconnecting from work			
Overload—fatigue and lack of focus over time on virtual			
Less effective team development—not able to connect and evolve as a team			
Technology challenges			

As you review your answers, think in solutions mode. What's working, and what is a workable solution for what is not?

Here are broader explanations of the challenges:

- **COMMUNICATION STRENGTH DIFFERENCES.** As with all aspects of CQ, communication strengths impact the effectiveness of virtual communication.

- **LESS FACE-TO-FACE.** We are human beings and value in-person connections. Remote communication can lead to a sense of loss and isolation. The water cooler and break room conversations are conducive to building relationships and to doing informal brainstorming during which, say, that next cost savings or innovation is imagined. The Pew Research Center reports that:
  - 60 percent of those surveyed say that working from home makes them feel less connected to coworkers.
  - 4 percent report feeling more connected.

  I was talking recently to a teacher who explained that virtual barriers negatively impacted her energy. She said: "I am kinesthetic when it comes to interacting with students. I can read them when we are physically together, and that just doesn't happen through a screen. It's all about being energized or having my energy, and ability to communicate and teach at the level my students deserve, diminished." This reality has impact across many environments. One of our clients recently made it policy for its emerging leaders to be in the physical office space a majority of the time. This is so they could experience firsthand the power of in-person interaction as an essential part of leaders' CQ. The nuances of non-verbal communication simply don't translate through a virtual screen. Many agree with the saying that *you can't replace face-to-face*.
- **LESS OR LESS EFFECTIVE FEEDBACK.** Feedback is an essential aspect of CQ. Receiving, giving, and following up takes more of an effort and intention in virtual environments.
- **PRESSURE TO STAND OUT—BIAS POTENTIAL.** An area of interest across the workspace continuum is whether there is a tendency (generally unintentional) of managers and colleagues to offer preferential treatment to those who are present in person. It can be a natural instinct to reach out to someone down the hall when a challenge or opportunity arises instead of arranging an online meeting. When it comes time for promotions or development plans, will the in-person employees be at the front of the line?

- **DISTRACTIONS.** Some of us are better at managing the unavoidable distractions of remote communication whether we are at home, at a coffee shop, or in another venue. We have all seen the videos of an interviewee interrupted by a toddler excited to climb on a parent's lap. Or the puppy who doesn't quite understand why his biped would prefer to look at a dumb screen than play and offer treats. There's the laundry, the garden, and (of course) more emails and social media. It takes intentional discipline and time management to get it all done effectively and efficiently and manage distractions.

- **DISCONNECTING.** If you have regular work hours in a traditional office environment—a nine-to-five or other shift—you can clock out at quitting time and (if your mindset and job description are so inclined) leave work tasks until the next day. It's not so easy if you get into the flow of virtual and digital work and hours pass without your taking a healthy break.

- **OVERLOAD.** How many virtual meetings can you take? It turns out that "Zoom fatigue" is a real deal. After three, four, or more online sessions in a day, it's natural to feel overwhelmed, and your communication and level of attention become less effective. In an hour-long virtual meeting, most participants will lose focus after the first 10 minutes. What's your experience?

- **LESS EFFECTIVE TEAM DEVELOPMENT.** It can be harder to connect and grow as a team. It takes different approaches to build and support teamwork online. How do you determine and measure team effectiveness when you are virtual or hybrid?

- **TECHNOLOGY CHALLENGES.** It probably goes without saying that a certain level of digital literacy is required to navigate the platform specifics and troubleshoot when challenges arise—especially when they happen "on the fly" in the middle of a meeting or presentation.

No doubt we will continue to learn more each day in the new work-*space*. I do look forward to five years from now reflecting on how the best practices have evolved.

COMMUNICATION STRENGTHS AND VIRTUAL ADAPTATION

Cocreation, collaboration, and creativity are being redefined in many industry sectors by online work. At the center of them all are our communication strengths. The digital applications that facilitate the processes performed by individuals are allowing new and convenient ways to accommodate unique workstyle preferences, roles, and needs. This flexibility in turn boosts productivity and innovation.

At the same time, how do you build a sense of community when you're perceived through a virtual and remote lens? The answer can be in understanding your communication strengths, how they translate in the virtual workspace, and how you can adapt to more effectively communicate with others.

CQ TIP. Consider your communication strengths as you review the tips below. In many cases, your related preferences and tendencies are magnified in the virtual world. What is emphasized through your verbal and nonverbal communication—e.g., with the focus on your face in the frame?

Tips for Optimizing Virtual CQ

Along with your list of advantages and challenges as well as your CQ strengths, here are a few tips to consider. Which ones would help you maximize advantages and mitigate challenges?

- **SCHEDULE IT.** If you don't schedule a virtual meeting, it won't happen. This may take an additional commitment and consideration of factors, such as time zones. Ensuring that invited participants know in advance the purpose and schedule of a meeting is the start of setting a solid foundation.
- **SET EXPECTATIONS.** Particularly if this is a meeting to get input or to make a decision (versus sharing information or directions), set expectations based on best practices. If you are a meeting organizer, this includes having an agenda, ensuring the right people are in

the room (e.g., decision makers if it's a "go or no-go" meeting), establishing rules of engagement (e.g., use chat, raise hands), and assigning facilitators and scribes. If you are a participant, this means being prepared, logging on early, having a focused mindset, and being responsible and respectful throughout the meeting.

- **BE PATIENT.** Technology happens! There will be internet challenges ("Your connection is unstable"), platform blips ("What happened with 'share screen'?"), and human error ("Do they know they are on mute?"). Take a deep breath, be helpful if it's appropriate, and smile.
- **BE INCLUSIVE.** There are a couple of levels when it comes to inclusivity in a virtual environment:
  - **Technology and access.** Don't assume that everyone understands how to navigate technology or has adequate access to the internet. This is an issue of equity that should be addressed. If there is a new employee, determining technology needs and training should be part of the onboarding process. Whenever virtual is introduced, ensuring employees have the tools and technology they need is a priority.
  - **Home or virtual workspace.** There may be those on the team who don't have a dedicated workspace or a home environment that is conducive to effective communicating. On a technological level, muting and having video turned off can be supportive if there is noise or other distractions in the background. Identifying workspace options, such as temporary office spaces or libraries with internet access, can be helpful.
- **REMEMBER THAT EVERYONE HAS A VOICE.** It is important that everyone have a voice in meetings designed to exchange information and elicit input. Awareness of CQ strengths and available tools (e.g., chat, raising hands, other emojis) can help achieve the goal that all feel welcome and that they belong.
- **REPEAT QUESTIONS.** Particularly in a hybrid environment, don't assume that all participants can hear well. Some may be positioned further away from a speaker in a physical room. Others may have

a hard time understanding a softer speaker. Whether a leader or participant, restating or rephrasing a question is a best practice. For example, "Damon's question was about the timeline for installing the new platform. The best answer I can offer right now is . . ."

- **USE VIRTUAL BODY LANGUAGE.** You're on candid camera! The impact of body language, particularly facial expressions, can be magnified in the Zoom room. Frame your face; make eye contact; smile. Frankly, it can be a mistake to turn your camera off, because the first thought is, "Where are they?" Yes, sometimes it is necessary; yet remember that "perception thing" and how you could be frustrating many of those on Zoom with you.

- **BUILD CONNECTIONS—WATER COOLER TIME.** How do you build connections when you're in virtual boxes? It's no secret that what many people miss about in-person communication is the interactions, the informal conversations, the opportunity to build community and connections. Maybe you can't exactly replicate the water cooler and break room banter, but you can allow time for connectivity and personalization. Appreciating the differences in communication styles and strengths is a good idea here. The patient individual may value extra time to understand and listen to others, whereas the impatient is counting the seconds to when he or she can jump to the next task.

- **TAKE BREAKS.** As mentioned above, attention spans can fade within the first 10 minutes or so of a virtual session, particularly if it's later in the workday or there have been multiple sessions. A good practice is for organizers to offer breaks, or for participants to agree to breaks— every 20 or 30 minutes is a good benchmark. In fact, there is a 20-20-20 guideline designed by optometrist Jeffrey Anshel. It suggests taking a 20-second break from the screen every 20 minutes by looking at something that is at least 20 feet away. This guideline is intended to help alleviate the stress on your eyes from staring at the computer.

- **GET IT HELP.** Everyone is going to need help with technology at some point. If you are in a leadership or influencer position in an organization, make sure that the IT staff and their contact information is known to employees. Any employee can try to get to know the IT personnel, who will be some of your best friends in the newer frontier. If you are a self-employed individual, you'll need to figure out whom can you call on who is dependable for assistance when it is needed.

It has never been more important to stay connected, get your message across effectively, and get your needs met in a timely manner. Accountability for *going to work* has been replaced with accountability for *doing the work,* and making sure that individuals and teams remain supported and connected is paramount.

ON THE ROAD TO CQ MASTERY—CONNECTING THROUGH VIRTUAL COMMUNICATION

Time to think forward and apply some of the learnings we know so far about virtual communication!

- Remote and hybrid workspaces are here to stay in some proportion and format.
- CQ is the most important competency for success in this newer frontier. It requires many of us to be aware of, and focus in on, challenges and opportunities.
- The next time you are positioned to engage in a remote work experience:
    - Be aware of your strengths and tendencies, as they are filtered and amplified by virtual communication.
    - Identify two or three areas where you can improve and be intent on these aspects.
    - Pay attention to how you interpret others' communication (including non-verbal) through the virtual lenses and features.
    - Be prepared to help others navigate and achieve their virtual potential.

- ○ Pay attention to personal preferences about how to interact if there is flexibility—e.g., would a customer prefer an in-person versus remote presentation?
- Invite your accountability partner to exchange observations and ideas on how to develop virtual CQ.
- If you're new to a virtual platform, consider a trial run with a colleague to test how your technology is working, how you come across, etc.

WHAT'S NEXT?

There's a reason that *earning and gaining trust* is the last chapter in a book on Communication Intelligence and the capstone of the CQ essentials. How do you earn trust? Turn the page and find out.

CHAPTER
17

CQ10: EARNING TRUST

As you earn and grant trust,
the dividends far exceed the investment.

Dorothy Spencer served as a team leader at the Tyson Foods processing plant in Neosho, Missouri, in the early 1990s. I had the privilege of working with her and learned lessons about trust that I will never forget.

Here's our story:

SITUATION. Dorothy led a team of 48 associates responsible for deboning and preparing chickens for "tray packs" for sale in grocery stores. The deboner job requires precise attention to detail and a high level of mental as well as physical dexterity. These associates work in wet, cold conditions in a high-paced environment. A challenge at the plant was that the team was experiencing high turnover—up to 50 percent in one month.

ACTION/RESULT. Utilizing the Forté Communicating to Hire and onboarding processes in a pilot program, Tyson realized a significant decrease in turnover, resulting in improved productivity and significant cost savings.

In research, a best practice is to have a control group so that you can compare results with what previously was being obtained. For the pilot, 25 percent of the team members were in a control group and did not receive Forté-related information.

LESSONS LEARNED ABOUT TRUST. Here was the interesting part. Every time Forté was able to reduce turnover, the production of the control group would come close to, or exceed, that of the treated group. This piqued my curiosity when I learned that Dorothy would gather the control group members at the end of the production line. I further observed that when the members of the control group performed exceptionally well during the week, Dorothy would take them to the Tyson cafeteria.

After the pilot was complete, I had the opportunity to have a private conversation with Dorothy, and here's what she shared:

- In the control group huddles, Dorothy would encourage the team members and give each a stick of Juicy Fruit gum.
- In the cafeteria meetings, she would congratulate members and buy each one a Coke.

After the pilot was concluded, the Forté process was introduced to Dorothy's team, and the results confirmed that the marriage of science and Dorothy's leadership style of "leading from the heart" and earning trust propelled results even higher. What Dorothy did was not in her job description. Dorothy was a true leader in every sense of the word who earned the trust of her team members through dedication, consistent communication, and empathy. She led from the heart and with sparks of ingenuity.

By the way, at the end of our conversation Dorothy gave me my own stick of Juicy Fruit and bought me a Coke. She said we had done a good job, too!

Even as I write this decades later, I tear up. Dorothy was one of the finest, most authentic, empathetic, and trustworthy leaders I have ever had the pleasure to work with.

KNOWING THE "WHAT AND WHY" OF TRUST WILL HELP GAIN AND MAINTAIN THIS KEY ELEMENT OF CQ! A well-accepted definition of trust is "the belief in the reliability, truth, ability, or strength of someone or something."

What does it take to be trustworthy? There's a reason why the topic of earning trust is the last chapter in this book on Communication Intelligence and caps off the list of the CQ ten essentials. Every one of the previous nine CQ essentials contributes to earning trust.

- Can you have trust without *clear, consistent communication*?
- Do *empathy* and *proactive listening* contribute to earning trust?
- What about a commitment to *expanding safe spaces* and to asking *meaningful questions*?
- *Receiving and giving feedback* and building bridges *when behavior is challenging* are ways to earn trust.
- Is maintaining trust challenging in a *virtual workspace*, and can interpretations of *non-verbal communication* impact trust?

The CQ thread through all the essentials weaves a durable and resilient fabric of trust . . . that is earned as well as granted.

WHERE ARE YOU NOW?

Where are you now in terms of understanding how to earn and grant trust?

LEVEL	DESCRIPTORS	WHERE I AM NOW
Novice	Either you have trust—or you don't. Is there more than that?	
Intermediate	I'm aware of how having trust (or not) impacts relationships and teams at work. I want people to trust me and to be confident in granting trust.	
Mastery	I work to earn the trust of others and grant trust when it is earned. When trust is broken (it happens), I focus on regaining trust and then maintaining it.	

In this chapter, you will:

- Confirm the *connection between CQ and trust*.

- Evaluate the *currency of earning trust.*
- Determine how to *regain trust* when it's broken.

COMMUNICATION INTELLIGENCE AND TRUST

Get out your highlighter—these critical learnings apply across your work and personal life!

"Just trust me." These three words should be near the top of the list of what *not* to say if you want to inspire trust in others. The speaker's intention could be tied to naivete, deception, or desperation. However, the impact is the opposite of engendering trust.

How long does it take to build trust? Although the exact length of time varies across research studies, there is consensus that it takes time—at least a number of months—to achieve a substantive level of trust.

How long does it take to break trust? Again, the research varies; however, all agree that it takes a much shorter time to break than build. Most of the people I've interviewed over decades say that it can "take a second" for a trusting relationship to be shattered.

How about rebuilding trust? It takes time—weeks, if not months—of consistent communication and actions, with the length depending on the parties involved and other factors.

At all stages of the equation, trust depends on Communication Intelligence on the part of the earner and the granter, as well as on the nature of the reciprocal relationship. When it is in place, the benefits are greater than the combination of the CQ essentials.

The Importance of Trust at Work

The importance of trust at work can't be understated:

- Trust leads to employees who feel that they are supported and that others have their back. This can be liberating! The resulting surplus of energy can result in increases in productivity, efficiency, and ingenuity.

- Employees who are truly trusted are more loyal to their organizations and team members. They are more likely to be engaged and stay in their jobs over time.
- Trust means colleagues have a sense of pride in what they do and are happier at work.

A low level of trust means higher turnover, lower productivity, and miserable morale. Without trust, workers can feel lost, unprotected, and even frightened. Are workers generally trusting of their employers? Edelman, a major public relations firm, has conducted the Edelman Trust Barometer for more than 20 years. Recent findings are that more than three-quarters of those surveyed trust their employer. Some may say that's pretty good news; however, there's room for improvement. Research shows that components of organizational trust include treating employees well, being open when a mistake is made, and performing in an ethical manner.

The Currency of Trust

When you look at most dictionary definitions of trust, the first entry will be about believing in the reliability and truth of someone or something. A second common definition has a financial connotation, as in "an arrangement in which someone's property or money is legally held or managed by someone else or by an organization (such as a bank) for usually a set period of time."

When you play out the money-trust metaphor, it starts to add up:

- **TRUST IS EARNED.** It is not something that automatically emerges when someone says those questionable words, "Just trust me." It's repeatedly demonstrating credibility and reliability. Do what you say you are going to do when you say you are going to do it! If, for some reason, you are not able to keep a commitment, own up to it as soon as possible and then reset.

   There is a debate about whether a successful trust transaction stems from earning trust or granting trust. In my experience, both sides of the ledger come into play, as this is a reciprocal arrangement. Yes, it's up to people to determine whether they will open the door to a trusting relationship. However, what is in your control is the investment you make in earning trust.

- **TRUST IS AN INVESTMENT.** Trust is an investment of the actions you choose to take over time. There's the integrity factor, which is demonstrating that you do what you say you are going to do. The most important overall factor is Communication Intelligence demonstrated on an ongoing basis.

- **TRUST PAYS GREAT DIVIDENDS.** The really good news is that trust is not just transactional; it's transformational. The results can be measured quantitatively in organizational and team outcomes. There also is a return on relationships that is measured in fundamentally human terms. What is the value of a relationship of mutual trust when you know that someone really understands you, accepts you, appreciates you for who you are, and will always have your back? The value is priceless. And you can take that to the bank!

In addition to the CQ essentials, there are two other factors to be added into the trust account:

- **DO YOU TRUST YOURSELF?** The answer to this question returns again to self-awareness. Are you overly dependent on what others think about you? Or, perhaps, do you find it very difficult to make even a simple decision? If you found yourself answering yes to either of the two previous questions, then you may want to take a tip from the great philosopher Michael Jackson and "start with the man in the mirror." Do your best, and give yourself a break instead of that negativity.

    CQ TIP. There is only one you out of the more than 100 billion people who have ever walked on the planet, and all you can do is be the best you at any point in time. If you don' trust yourself, would you expect others to find you trustworthy?

- **TRUST TO DO WHAT?** The truth is that trust is not necessarily an all-encompassing sweep of one's capability and reliability. A common response to the question about whether you trust someone is "to do what?" You may trust the math teacher to help students learn arithmetic but not necessarily to drive the school bus. The financial whiz is trustworthy when it comes to doing accounting but not to performing heart surgery.

CQ TIP. It is important in the trust equation to know what you trust someone to do . . . and not to do. And that includes yourself.

BREAKING TRUST

"I didn't mean to . . ." This can be the automatic reaction when people become aware that their communication and behavior translates into another not trusting them. There is some truth to the statement because many times we're not aware that we've broken the barrier.

In some cases, it traces back to communication strengths. For example, one with non-conformist tendencies may be focusing on the big picture and not include details that the conformist business partner needs to be comfortable. The conformist may interpret this as a trust breaker. The impatient person may see the patient counterpart as being slow and even lazy and not worthy of trust to get a task done quickly enough.

In other cases, the trust perceiver may not be in an empathetic frame of mind or may not listen all the way through. For example, let's say a colleague uncharacteristically shows up late for a meeting. Without finding out any information about the backstory, an associate determines she is not trustworthy. The truth is that there is a sick child at home who was in need of care in this one-off instance.

Then there are the more obvious signals of broken trust—individuals may lie repeatedly or not live up to a commitment that was made. Organizations may prioritize profit over people or reverse course on promises (e.g., cancel vacation days or renege on a promised bonus). This is another case when the perceiver's truth is the reality. If someone believes trust is broken, it's up to that individual to address it. Now, what if someone has no desire to ever correct mistakes or own up to fixing trust? Is there anything you can say to someone who is thinking that? Clearly, you hope the person is open to a coaching moment; yet some people just will not do it. Needless to say, this will derail the person's career, and your time as a colleague or leader is best spent on those who are open to listen and evolve.

Reasserting Trust

When trust is broken, there are certain steps you can take to regain it:

- **SEEK TO UNDERSTAND.** This may involve having a difficult conversation, asking good questions, proactively listening, and looking to find common ground.
- **OWN IT!** If you contributed to the trust breach, admit it promptly. This could be with an external customer. For almost all customers and clients I've worked with, proactive communication is the number one factor tied to trust. So own it when, for example, an order has been delayed, or when the breach is related to an internal customer or team: "I recognize that I had the wrong information in the presentation. I deeply apologize and can promise it won't happen again. What can I do now to repair the damage?"
- **ALLOW EMOTIONS TO SURFACE.** In many situations when trust is broken, the damage unleashes emotions that run strong and deep. The breach may have triggered feelings in a colleague from a situation that isn't directly related—for example, that colleague's father may have lied repeatedly when the colleague was young, and your omission feels like revictimization. Even if it's uncomfortable, it will likely accelerate progress toward re-earning trust if you allow the other party to express and vent.
- **INVEST IN RE-EARNING TRUST.** This is a more intense variation on initially earning trust in that, particularly in the time frame shortly after the infraction, your every move will be closely watched. Even the slightest hint of a rebreak may move the trust ledger backward and not forward. This will take repeated actions over time that follow the integrity formula of doing what you say you're going to do when you say you're going to do it.
- **COMMUNICATE.** It comes full circle back to communication, doesn't it? In the case of regaining trust, the best advice is to err on the side of

more communication than less. And then check for understanding. So state what you will do, do what you say, and then check to ensure that the action is acknowledged. Over and over again.

ON THE ROAD TO MASTERY—EARNING TRUST

I hope that along the journey of Communication Intelligence, there have been multiple opportunities for you to consider, reflect, and act in ways that lead you toward CQ mastery, including those related to trust. The choices you make now and in the future about earning and granting trust are, perhaps, among the most important you will make in your professional and personal life.

The great Russian playwright Anton Chekhov said, "You must trust and believe in people or life becomes impossible." When I think back on all the people whom I have trusted, and who have trusted me over the decades, I still think of Dorothy Spencer and how she made her team members believe and know they belonged by earning their trust. I suddenly have a craving for Juicy Fruit gum and a Coke. Would you care to join me?

WHAT'S NEXT?

That's the question at the heart of the next few pages—the road to your CQ mastery continues.

YOUR COMMUNICATION INTELLIGENCE JOURNEY CONTINUES

In introducing you to the Communication Intelligence journey, I suggested it would be a time of discovery during which you would learn more about yourself and your relation to others. I shared my interest in CQ that began when I was a kid and that evolved into The Forté Institute and a lifelong commitment to help others improve communication, collaboration, and the quality of work and life.

Along the way, you have so far been prompted to take and document actions that make sense for you now—and in the future—in order to advance your CQ proficiency. I hope you considered inviting an accountability partner along for the ride. You may recall that research shows that when you have dedicated check-in conversations with a trusted friend or colleague, it is 95 percent likely that you will achieve your objectives.

It was noted that, over the course of the CQ journey, practices may evolve into habits. Have you begun to experience the world of work and others a little differently as your self-awareness and situational awareness evolve, for example, around your CQ strengths? Are you more dialed into the communication strengths of those you interact with and the way you need to adapt your behavior? Have others noted that your communications have positively impacted your relationships and the work environment?

I didn't promise it would all be easy. It wouldn't be surprising if you paused at different stages, unsure of the significance of your CQ evolution. My hope is that you then stepped up to accept the next challenge and opportunity. And I hope you have had a little fun along the ride so far.

Now I have an important question to ask. It's the same one I posed at the beginning of the CQ journey. *Where are you now on the road to CQ mastery?* Use the table to find out.

Where am I on the Communication Intelligence Continuum?		
Name: _____ Date:_____		
LEVEL	**DESCRIPTION**	**WHERE I AM NOW**
Novice	I have a basic understanding of effective ways of communicating at work. I am curious about what causes effective communication and miscommunication. I would like to learn how to improve my communication.	
Intermediate	I can describe examples of how communication impacts work—positively and negatively. I have read about differences in the ways people communicate. I have, on occasion, tried to improve my communication abilities.	
Mastery	I can explain to others what Communication Intelligence is and why it is important. I understand my Communication Intelligence strengths and how others perceive me. I take action on a daily basis to evolve my Communication Intelligence.	

LIFELONG CQ LEARNING

You picked up this book for a reason. My guess is that it wasn't because someone paid you to check it out or that you will receive an educational degree. It was because you wanted to learn more about CQ, how to be your best, and how to bring your best to work and life. You were drawn to invest your time and energy in the most important asset you have—you!

As a practitioner of lifelong learning, you likely recognize the benefits that occur when you choose to explore, act, and grow personally and professionally. There are demonstrated advantages in terms of improving communication (the most important competency now and in the future), confidence, and personal fulfillment. It may position you for career advancement and likely makes you a better resource to help others learn and grow.

The good news, then, is that you can choose to continue the CQ journey. As you reflect on what you have learned and accomplished so far, what are three areas that come to mind? These could be related to CQ strengths, the CQ 10 essentials, or any one of the strategies and tips you may have selected to advance your personal journey. They likely are actions that have helped improve relationships at work and that you have shared with others. Take this opportunity to make a note or two below—we remember best what we write down. Also, this creates a "benchmark" to continue your growth cycle.

_____

_____

_____

_____

_____

Moving forward, consider doing these three things as you continue the journey:

- Review areas of the book that you are still curious about and would like to investigate more in depth than the first time around.
- Check in with your accountability partner about your next chapter.
- Drop me a note. I'd love to hear your story or answer your questions (cq@theforteinstitute.com).

And now I have one important question for you—what's next?

ACKNOWLEDGMENTS

This book could never have happened without the support of so many individuals contributing their ideas and suggestions over the development and continual improvement of how we best communicate and adapt with one another. You know who you are; I am eternally in your debt. While the journey began in the mid-1970s, the evolution of Forté is as recent as yesterday.

All those who have ever taken a Forté, or will take a Forté or an Adapting Update, receive an email from us the next day asking them to rate the validity of their report and add any comments/suggestions they would like. Their responses are solid gold to us and help continually improve Forté.

When McGraw Hill approached me about writing this book, it had been a long-term Forté client. I was both flattered and humbled. Senior Editor Cheryl Segura has made this process clear and easy to understand and has been an invaluable partner every step of the way. Senior Marketing Manager Scott Sewell and developmental editor Meghan Hurley-Powell cannot be thanked enough for their help and guidance along the way.

It takes a team, and Rae Nelson and Karl Haigler of Haigler Enterprises have led the way with boundless energy and intellect, besides being Forté Thought Leaders for over a decade. Dr. Rick Olson, Forté Thought Leader, and Jessica Wolfe, Director of Forté Client Success, were integral as well.

As the focus is on the practical aspects of Communication Intelligence, teachings from real-world experiences are woven throughout the pages. Special thanks to Deb Sinta, Tommy Geary, Dr. Cynthia DeVita-Cochrane,

Kim Ramsey, Col. Rob Campbell, Don Brown, Dr. Larry Long, Lori Harris, Bob Pious, John Weeks, Tom Mitchell, Gemma Smith, Lynn Whitesell, Kathryn Findlen, Leslie Farias, Dr. Chris Neibauer, Amryl Ward, Terry Clark, Al Ragland, Anita Brick, Sam Weber, Bob Eaton, Sheriff Ed McMahon, Joel Dannelley, Cheryl Morlote, Anne Keeble, Dr. Douglas Waldrep, Annie Dee, Rachel Olsen, Michelle Markey, Tony Herrin, Amy Moran-Moberg, Stephen Dowd, Ross Thornton, Dr. Joe Green, Harry Florio, Jr., the late Rob Berkley, Bill Ayers, Gary Agnew, Mike Hazell, Nancy Johnson, Brid Bourke, Simon McAuliffe, YouMe Jeon, Sohyun Kim, Hisyam Omar, Anthony Raja Devadoss, and, as you have read, Dorothy Spencer.

INDEX

ABOUT THE AUTHOR

C. D. "HOOP" MORGAN, III, is the founder and chairman of The Forté Institute, LLC, a global behavioral sciences firm best known for developing and providing innovative people, process, and interpersonal performance-improvement solutions.

Photo credit: Cody Milewski of Cassian Films

Hoop is an internationally recognized expert in Communication Intelligence™ and has devoted almost five decades to optimizing the CQ of individuals, leaders, and teams.

He is the author and developer of the proprietary, computerized Forté Interpersonal Communication Style Profile, which is used throughout the world.

Forté has served 6 million people at over 6,000 companies including Microsoft, LinkedIn, Berkshire Hathaway Energy, PERSOLKELLY, Tyson Foods, Ace Hardware, GMC, Aflac, Amazon, Bank of America, Citi Group, Dell, Deloitte, Google, Harvard Business School, KPMG, Motorola, Pfizer, and more.

Morgan is a graduate of Missouri Southern State University. His educational background includes studies at the Sloan School of Management and at Harvard Law School.